Acclaim for Asskickonomics

"I'm a voracious reader of business books, so when I got *Asskickonomics*, I instantly took time to devour it. Kristen has taken her experience and distilled it down into an easy-to-understand success manual. The specifics she tackles regarding procrastination and the inability to finish projects will get you on the fast track to finishing what you start."

David L. Hancock, Founder, Morgan James Publishing

"If you're ready to stop dreaming and start living the life you've always wanted, this book gives you the map AND the mindset. If you're brave enough to take on the challenge, you'll recognize this book as the key difference maker when you look back on your life 5 years from now. Get it. Read it. Take action on it!"

Jim Edwards, The Jim Edwards Method

"When it comes to your success... there is only one person responsible for making it happen: YOU! *Asskickonomics* is the practical guidebook for developing the self-discipline needed to experience the level of income and achievement that you crave and deserve. When you master the ability to kick your own ass into action you simultaneously master the ability to manifest your dreams. Get the book. Implement the strategies. Enjoy the abundance that *Asskickonomics* naturally brings into your life."

Daniel Hall, host of the RealFastResults.com Podcast

"Yikes! Kristen has some tough talk for entrepreneurs who are wondering why they aren't where they want to be. But in addition to the rip-the-bandage-off tough love, she shares how to get past the most common problem of what she calls the 'Normalcy Trap' to finally reach the goals your heart desires. Vulnerable, fun, inspiring, stinging, motivating, and helpful—you'll find what you need to get going and find success."

Felicia J. Slattery, M.A., M.Ad.Ed., Author of Kill the Elevator Speech

"I love this stuff!! For over two decades I've both taught and studied what it takes to be a successful entrepreneur. When you work with as many people as I have, you start to recognize the patterns that it takes to be a great entrepreneur.

In her new book *Asskickonomics*, Kristen Joy Laidig gives you the exact patterns that it takes to cut and shape yourself into the genius entrepreneur that's already within you, waiting to shine!

Not only does she show you how to get focused and handle the distractions but you'll also be shown how to kick self-sabotages' butt in a downright practical, long lasting way. Two thumbs up for writing the book that should be mandatory reading for every entrepreneur and soon to be entrepreneur."

Ty Cohen, Founder of WritersLife.org

"If you'd like to stop wasting time and start building the business and life of your dreams, you'll want to know about *Asskickonomics* by Kristen Joy Laidig. Kristen has made herself a student of success who has grown her business to a place that many can barely imagine. In *Asskickonomics,* she unveils powerful success strategies that can change your business, your life, your income and the trajectory of your destiny.

You'll love Kristen's writing style. This is not one of those typical, dry, boring, business books. Rather, this book takes us on a journey and is filled with compelling stories that makes it difficult to put the book down. Pick up a copy today and learn how to stop spinning your wheels and start achieving your dreams."

D'vorah Lansky, M.Ed., Bestselling Author,
ShareYourBrilliance.com

"I tore through *Asskickonomics*... as if my life depended on it. Kristen's easy writing style, humorous stories, and business lessons are pure mind bombs. I can't imagine a better book about KICKING ASS in any new business!"

John S. Rhodes, Best-Selling Author and Founder of WebWord

"Kristen Joy Laidig's *Asskickonomics* is a much-needed wake-up call for 'wantrepreneurs' seeking to become successful, legit entrepreneurs. Her straight talk and practical ideas will knock you out of your 'Normalcy Trap,' show you exactly what you need to do to get out of your own way, and demonstrate how to harness your Upper Realm, Inner Realm and Lower Realm to finally achieve the dreams that have long been eluding you."

Lou Bortone, Recovering Wantrepreneur and
Author of Video Marketing Rules!

"*Asskickonomics* is now my new go-to book when I need a serious kick in the butt to get my life back on track. Kristen does an amazing job of smashing through the thought patterns that keep most of us stuck in a life of 'normalcy' and reveals exactly how to make subtle changes in your thinking to take ownership of every important aspect of your life.

At around page 32 it all hit home for me and it likely will for you too. Kristen slices right through the pre-concieved notions you cling to, while showing you how to make these things work in your favor to structure a much happier, more successful life. This is POWERFUL stuff.

Asskickonomics will give you real clarity and understanding of how to take ownership of each challenge life brings you whether in business or personal. It will teach you how to easily turn obsticles into catapults. Most importantly, it will give you a total sense of, 'I can do this.' A brilliant book by a brilliant author. Thank you Kristen!"

Gene Pimentel, MarketersAdvantage.com

"An insanely fun book that will show you how to succeed in business and life. If you're ready to kick some ass as an entrepreneur and create a business that makes a difference, you'll love *Asskickonomics*."

Tom Corson-Knowles, Founder of TCK Publishing

"Smart. Fun. Engaging. Kristen knows a thing or two about business and overall success in general.

This book cuts through the normal generic advice and offers a personal view on what it takes to succeed in business/entrepreneurship today.

Open your heart and pay close attention. Kristen unlocks a lot of mystery and tells it like it is."

Rory F. Stern, Founder RFS Digital Media

"From the opening paragraph to the last Kristen Joy Laidig lays out a solid plan that every business owner and entrepreneur should read and internalize. Kristen says in the book, "Here's a news flash for you… nothing is new. Everything has already been done before." Although there is some truth to that, it's how you add value to what has been done before and make it better that counts.

What Kristen does is take some tried and true business concepts and organizes them in a new way that makes them easy to consume, digest, and execute.

She talks about Trickle Down Asskickonomics and how to avoid the Normalcy Trap, understanding your Upper, Inner, and Lower Realms (spheres of influence for your success), and a clear example of finding your 'Why" and taking action.

The wisdom and stories in this book are engaging, practical, and spot on. You will *definitely* want to read this book more than once, since success is a journey, not a destination. This is not a road map as much as a tour guide of stops along the way. Get going today and start kicking ass!"

Brian Basilico, Author, Speaker, Strategist

ASS
KICK
ONOMICS

The Powerful Unseen Force
Behind Every Successful Entrepreneur!

KA-POW!

Kristen Joy Laidig

gréine
PUBLICATIONS

CHAMBERSBURG, PA

Published by Gréine Publications in 2018

Chambersburg, Pennsylvania

First edition; First printing

Layout, design and writing ©2018 Kristen Joy Laidig

Cover design by Tony Laidig

ISBN 978-1-941638-14-9

To the entrepreneurs who are ready to level up and kick serious ass in their businesses.

Table of Contents

Foreword

Another book on personal development for entrepreneurs? Do we truly need it, when there are thousands of other books flooding the market?

And the answer is a resounding YES! For three reasons.

The first of which being the fact that you are sitting here right now with this book in your hands. If you didn't need another personal development book, then why are you reading these words right now? Chances are, it is because you have not found the one piece of advice that makes it all "click" for you. That one little bit that will help you overcome challenges, adversities, and all the mental trash filling up your head that prevents you from taking action and getting shit done.

The second reason this book is needed is because this book is *different* in its approach. Whereas most personal development books focus on broad, overarching ideas and giving your nice little feel-good warm fuzzies, *Asskickonomics* instead focuses on the tangible, real world areas of your life that you need to deal with *and* gives you practical tools and strategies to deal with them.

And that is why I love this book and agreed to write this Foreword. I am all about taking fast, imperfect action in both life and business and it has served me well over the years. I also love to read and learn, but nothing irritates me more than reading a book full of great sounding ideas that gives me no practical way to implement and take action.

Because as we all know knowledge is nothing without execution. In the following chapters, you will be equipped with the tools you need to execute on everything you learn.

Now before we go on, let me back up really quick and introduce myself. My name is Tanner Larsson and I am a self-admitted serial entrepreneur. I have started, stopped, co-founded, built, sold, scaled, bankrupted, closed, failed and/or succeeded with over two dozen different companies in my career.

I have produced a couple hundred million dollars in revenues for multiple companies in a wide variety of industries. Through this, I have experienced the myriad pendulum swings an entrepreneur goes through as they take on the world.

I also have the great privilege of running a high-level mastermind group full of the best and brightest online entrepreneurs on the planet. It was through this mastermind that I first met Kristen when she joined with her husband Tony. One of the first things I noticed about them was how quickly and effectively they overcame obstacles that came up in their businesses. Many entrepreneurs get bogged down by obstacles, and despite running both online and offline businesses at the same time, Kristen and Tony were able to motor through and keep their businesses growing.

Which brings me to the third reason this book is needed and probably the most important reason as to why you should read it.

All the training, tweaks, hacks, systems, strategies, and shortcuts you accumulate don't mean a thing (and won't help you a bit) until you first become aware of the biggest problem in your business.

This problem is the biggest success preventer you'll ever have to deal with and it's responsible for derailing practically every business in existence. So, what is this huge problem?

You are not going to like the answer. Because the answer is... YOU! You, the entrepreneur, are the destroyer of your own business success.

And nobody else on Earth can do as much consistent, ongoing, and never-ending damage to your business that you will do.

Ouch, right?

Think I'm being too harsh?

Don't believe me?

It's ok. The first time this was pointed out to me, I didn't believe it either.

In fact, I got pissed off at my mentor Vinnie Fisher and told him in a less than polite tone that I'm *not* the problem in my business because I am the only one making it work... making it pay, that all these "other things" are the real problem. My response, while entirely rude, was also completely expected by Vinnie.

It's the natural, knee jerk reaction of an entrepreneur to look at themselves as the knight in shining armor that is saving their business from all the outside problems affecting it.

But the reality is that most of those problems are caused by the human inside that shiny armor.

These problems are all problems of the mind and this "mental trash" is what entrepreneurs have to fight through every single day of their lives.

Inside *Asskickonomics*, Kristen takes you through a systematic and insightful process of eliminating this mental trash from your life so you can truly succeed with your business.

So, grab a cup of coffee, find a quiet place and get ready to have your ass kicked!

Tanner Larsson

Author of *Ecommerce Evolved: The Essential Playbook To Build, Grow & Scale A Successful Ecommerce Business*

Introduction

What's wrong with a lot of entrepreneurs today? They jump from "business" opportunity to "business" opportunity because that next one is a "sure thing." From that hot trendy software tool you could be an affiliate for to that shiny network marketing company that promises five figures in 30 days. From project idea to a new project when the first one isn't even half finished. Maybe it's because they're still searching for their passion. Or maybe, as I truly believe, they're just lazy. Not the sit-on-your-ass-and-eat-bonbons-and-watch-TV kind of lazy, but rather the do-as-little-as-it-takes-to-keep-up-with-the-Joneses-but-never-really-make-it kind of lazy. The kind of lazy that's always keeping them one step behind their goals and one step closer to burnout and frustration. The kind that makes it easy for them to hop on to the next "this is *guaranteed* to make you rich" scheme. The kind that keeps them from having to be responsible for their *success,* because then they'll have to own how awesome they truly are, and it's frankly easier to stay miserably "almost" successful.

Can you relate? Do you find yourself jumping from half-finished idea to new ideas, whether it's a project idea or that new supplement company, and right when things get to the point that you actually have to do more than the bare minimum to see any sort of cash flow you find something *else* that's better to become the "expert" in? Or maybe you're still searching for that *one* thing you can get truly passionate about? *Or*, as I really believe is the case with most entrepreneurs, deep down do you actually *know* your unique purpose, but running headlong fully into it scares the living shit out of you?

YOU ARE RESPONSIBLE FOR YOUR OWN SUCCESS

The fact is *you* are responsible for your own decisions, your own failures, and most importantly, your *own success*. And that's enough to scare *anybody*. It's why it took me a year and a half to start writing this book after I first got the idea. I've known deep down that this message is my higher purpose and calling, to ass-kick-inspire *want*repreneurs to get off their excuses and take action to be *real, successful* entrepreneurs. But I had to create a program called the Book Writing Challenge to get off *my* ass and take action and write this book. I had to ask my best friend to hold me accountable to get it done. And when we discovered that wasn't enough motivation, we got the idea to bring a group of people together and hold each other accountable to finish our "heart-want" book idea projects over the course of six months. It took the potential public humiliation of not getting this book finished to motivate me even to *start* the project. And I started the international brand *The Book Ninja*... I should be able to say, "I got this!" and just run with it, right?!

Here's a little secret... You're not meant to do this business thing alone! Whatever your ideas for projects, product lines, services, etc., you're not meant to sit by yourself in your closet and piddle away each day making a couple of social media posts and hoping the money rolls in. You're designed to share your success—and failures—with others. You're designed to allow others to help you to gain clarity with your ideas. You're designed to *take action*, but *not alone!*

To illustrate this point, let me tell you a little story about how one of my mentors almost lost his life and how a little thing I call Trickle-Down Asskickonomics® saved it.

What is Trickle-Down Asskickonomics?

Trickle-Down Asskickonomics is the most powerful form of ass kicking there is. In fact, seeing this phenomenon unfold in person is actually what inspired this entire book.

I was sitting in a mastermind session listening to our leader Tanner talk about how he got his ass kicked. One of his products was performing poorly in sales, and before trashing it altogether his team decided to try one more thing to save it. Within a few *hours*, that part of his business blew up. Suddenly they were sold out of the product and within a couple of weeks they were back ordered six months with the manufacturer. It grew so fast they had to get a bigger warehouse and more employees, and they still didn't have the capability to handle the load. He started funding inventory from his own personal income, and while money was coming in from the product sales, they had to advance-purchase inventory, handle payroll, and other overhead costs that were slowly draining his personal accounts. Tanner had stumbled upon a highly successful part of his business, and it was so successful so fast that he literally nearly had a heart attack.

I could see how it was hard for him to share his vulnerabilities with the group as his experience and subsequent hospital visit showed with raw emotion on his face. *His* mentor, Vinnie, was sitting next to him, and he shared how he flew to Tanner's house and sat with him on his kitchen floor as he struggled with what to do... in the midst of unexpected chest pain. Tanner was young, physically fit (like crazy fit), and ate super healthy, so there was *no reason* he should be showing symptoms of a heart attack… yet there it was.

I sat on the edge of my seat as Tanner shared his story. I watched in awe as both these men who'd made more money in one day than I'd made in my most profitable month thus far exposed their struggles. Then Vinnie spoke up about how he helped Tanner to see how he created this scenario, how to fix it, and what to do if it happened again… And gave him a royal ass kicking from the Upper Realm of Asskickonomics *not to let it happen again.*

What surprised me even more than Tanner's vulnerable baring of his struggles was when Vinnie shared how he got *his* ass kicked… by one of his employees. A man who another time lost more money on a single business deal than I had thus far made in a month. He told the story of how he had recently invested over $50,000 on a new project and was just ready to "push the button" and make it "live" when one of his employees asked a simple question… "Please explain to me how this project fits into our mission and vision for the company?" Silence. He stopped, stared, and in that moment realized that the new project did not align with the company goals and vision, but rather it was a costly distraction that pulled it *away* from its vision. Ten seconds and 50k later, that project was scrapped. Just reading this story might make you think he was out of his mind. After all, who in their right mind would literally throw away in a few seconds more money than most Americans make in a year? It wasn't that he has endless resources… it's that his openness to the Lower Realm of Asskickonomics allowed him to listen to an employee's concerns. This openness helped him to get clear on his purpose and vision, and when he made the mistake that started to pull him and everyone working with and for him away from that vision, he was willing to let it go.

Vinnie understood how much that project would have cost in manpower and resources to keep running and how it would have taken away from the company's core objective. But even more importantly, he understood the rule of Trickle-Down Asskickonomics.

Trickle-Down Asskickonomics is the ability to hold yourself to your goals, with or without others holding you accountable (the Inner Realm). It's also the ability to be open to feedback and accountability from the Upper Realm (those above you in authority) and the Lower Realm (those below you in authority). And most importantly, it's the ability to know when you've made a mistake, re-evaluate where you're headed and what's needed to get there, and *listen* to smart people around you rather than immediately getting defensive when they bring up something you don't want to hear... especially if that smart person is an "underling."

The power behind Asskickonomics is the willingness to get your ass kicked and to take it with grace, and it's the secret that makes successful entrepreneurs change their lives and accomplish their dreams.

In fact the "secret" to success isn't a secret at all. It's simple Trickle-Down Asskickonomics. Tanner's mentor understood what it *really* takes to be successful... to play in all three realms simultaneously. While he was in the process of kicking Tanner's ass, Vinnie was open to his employee kicking his.

If your ass is being kicked by someone not willing to have *his or hers* kicked, it's time for you to get a new mentor, as you've removed the trickle-down equation from Asskickonomics and it will not be nearly as effective. Because all successful people know there's really only *one* reason they're successful. They're being held accountable to their goals, their dreams, and their words... by themselves, their mentors, and anyone assisting in making those goals reality... activating the powerful Trickle-Down Effect.

In this book I'm going to pull you out of the whirlwind you've become comfortable with, the "normal" that has become your daily existence, into the new territory of Asskickonomics so we can build a solid foundation of what it really takes to be successful.

You may not like some of the things I say, and that's OK. Some of my points may piss you off, and that's OK too. In fact if something in this book doesn't make you uncomfortable, I haven't done my job to help you stretch and grow. And growth is the key to get past entrepreneurial "survival" mode and to build a wildly successful, thriving business. If you're happy with constantly living in survival mode and that normalization is OK with you, put this book down. I won't hold anything against you for doing so; I know you'll pick it back up when you're ready. And if you're ready to thrive and be as productive and financially successful as the business owners you envy, keep reading.

1

Idea vs. Action

Let's face it, life constantly throws us curve balls. One minute everything is great, the next we've hit an all-time low and suddenly we're living in a van down by the river. This is what I call the *Normalcy Trap*. Human beings inherently don't like change. In fact we despise it. Whether good or bad, change makes us uneasy because it's outside what we've deemed as normal. When something amazing happens, we find a way to self-sabotage it out of our lives to get back to what we're familiar with as being normal. Either we start to think that we don't deserve it, we're not good enough for it, or sometimes it's a completely unintentional act of our subconscious that pulls us back to our normal.

While I was growing up a common phrase my mom used was, "Normal is a setting on a dryer." She meant that our family was a little nuts, and that humans in general have their quirks. However as I've grown and my life has shifted as I've uncomfortably embraced the pain of change, I've realized this phrase reaches much farther than our human "weirdness." It tells the truth of life itself. Life is not normal, yet we continuously try to cram our lives into the box of normalcy. Someone offers us a bigger box and we shove it away because it's different. We resist the gift of a compliment because our norm is to put ourselves down.

Recently I had the opportunity to grow. A shift happened, and I had to choose whether to step into it or to close my tiny normal box and keep the change at bay. I've learned over the past several years that when it comes to personal and business growth, not only are the two interrelated and play off one another, but also when I embrace one, while it's usually uncomfortable going through the process, it feels amazing on the other side. I had a revelation that I put myself down as a form of punishment for being smart. All my life in school I was punished for being smart. My third-grade teacher called me stupid in front of the entire class and sent me to the principal's office... because I was so bored I doodled all over my homework. In high school I was punished by a teacher because I got all my work done in study hall and never took home any homework. And in college a professor told me I would "never make it in the *real* world" because I would never be "good enough" no matter how hard I worked.

My messed-up Normalcy-Trap brain started to believe I was stupid and to prove that belief I made stupid decisions and surrounded myself with people who were not brilliant entrepreneurs... Then I would complain about those people when it was all me punishing myself because I believed "stupid" was my normal! I'm not saying that's not messed up... and yet that's exactly what our subconscious mind does. It believes something, establishes that "fact" as normal, and then does everything in its power to keep us there until we become so uncomfortable in our state of normal that we have to find a *new* normal.

To steal another old saying of my mother's, "Until the pain of staying the same is *greater* than the pain of change, you won't change." This has been proven in my life many times over, and I'm sure in yours as well. How bad does it have to hurt before you visit a doctor? How hard does work have to get before you seek out another stream of income? How nasty does that client have to be before you fire him? In both life and business it's incredibly easy to fall into the Normalcy Trap... and live there. In fact most aspiring entrepreneurs never make it out!

For many entrepreneurs normal means struggle, hunger, and constantly striving for that "next big thing." When that next big thing hits, before we know it, we're out of money. A joke in our household is that we challenge anyone to spend money as fast as we can. When we've had business home runs, it's not unusual for our accounts to go from a $50,000 payday down to a $1,000 balance within 48 hours, which makes us seek out that next payday as fast as we can. As Doug Brackmann and Randy Kelley wrote in their book *Driven*, "One big payday should not change your standard of living dramatically. It is incredibly easy to sabotage with money... We are hunters designed to live in a world without refrigerators. We kill it. Eat it. Get hungry. Go kill another one. When we're financially secure, we lose our hunger, so we spend until we're hungry again."

They sum up the Normalcy Trap phenomenon well. Until we have a consistent run of big paydays, that standard is not normal to us and our subconscious is constantly being driven to normalize.

> **NORMAL DOES NOT HAVE TO EQUAL STRUGGLE, HUNGER, AND LACK OF MONEY**

This struggle presents itself often in the entrepreneur's finances and also in personal health and relationships.

My Normalcy Trap

Two weeks before Christmas I hired a personal trainer to help me get back in shape for the holidays. And while he did help me get back in shape, he also helped me with an issue I thought I was doomed to have my entire life. For as long as I can remember my knees have faced each other and I always walked (and ran) funny. This defect, which I thought I'd had since birth, was the source of a lot of torment and emotional abuse from schoolmates, not to mention literal pain in my legs and hips. I learned to live with it… with the normalcy… in constant, chronic pain. And any treatment that claimed it could help me took me away from my normalcy of pain, which felt unusual, so I would get injured and end up hurting again. That is until a personal trainer named Glenn showed up in my life and said, "I can fix you."

While I don't believe I was inherently broken or anything, the idea that my "defect," the "normal" I had lived with my entire life, could be "fixed" was intriguing. And yet it still took me almost two *years* to take Glenn up on his offer to fix me. I was scared. Scared of what the new normal would mean for all the excuses I gave not to do something physical that I just didn't want to do. I'd gotten so used to my Normalcy Trap I had a freaking zip code in Painville, and I used it to my advantage to get out of anything I didn't want to do. In fact the only reason I thought about working with Glenn was because the pain of staying the same got so intense that I couldn't handle it anymore. And then it *still* took *him* reaching out to *me* for me to say, "Yes, I'll let you train me."

Until I actually put my money where my mouth was and hired him, it was just an idea… one that didn't do anything positive for my body until it became more than a passing thought. Once I took *action* on that idea, I saw results. Mega. Results. Within two *days* my left knee was almost straight. It was so fast and shocking that I struggled with this new normal. I kept looking at my knee, wondering how fast it would turn back in… every morning for weeks! About a month later, my chronic hip pain was almost totally gone. And two months later? I'd dropped 30lbs, from pushing a Size 14 to a Size 8, and went from what he called "knocked knees to knockout." It was a transformational experience that I'll always remember, and the constant pain I'd learned to live with as my "normal" standard became a distant memory as a new normal of straight legs and painless walking took hold. In fact it's become such a distant memory that while I sometimes still gaze at my straightened legs in wonder, those moments are becoming fewer as I live every day with this new normal.

Then after our three-month training regimen was over, I stopped working with him. Two months after I stopped training with him as I sit here and write this chapter, I realize I've slipped off my healthy eating plan. My workout routine is almost nonexistent. And my waistline? Expanded. I'm once again at a point of frustration, but not because of physical pain. Now I'm facing an entirely new set of personal development challenges and I have to make the choice *again...* what will be my normal?

My Choice to Succeed or Not to Succeed

Did my latest weight gain occur because I was on some sort of yo-yo fad diet and fell off the bandwagon? Not unless you count eating real food and decreased sugar a "fad" diet... which I don't. Is it because I stopped working out? I'm sure that was part of it. I've had every legitimate excuse in the book to back away from my healthy habits... from opening a toy store to renovations on our house to spending time writing this book. I mean, any *normal* person under that kind of stress would slip and gain 20lbs back, right?!

The fact is I know myself pretty well. I know I'm like most other human beings in that to stick with my goals long term, I *need* accountability, and I need to set new standards of normalcy. No one was meant to walk this path of humanity and discovery alone. We're all meant to have *someone* we can turn to, someone who can point out to us our own personal silliness and hand us a bigger box. Whether that's a coach, a mentor, or an accountability partner—sometimes it takes an external force to keep us joined at the hip with our dreams. Because without any form of accountability, our ideas will forever remain ideas. Without someone handing us the bigger box or the better mousetrap and changing the normalcy of our ideas staying as just ideas, we'll stay stuck in the trap. It's only once we have a big enough reason to take action on those ideas, to make that change and break out of the trap of normalcy, that we see any sort of success. And that reason could be a looming deadline, a self-imposed goal, a high-school reunion or wedding, or just being so freaking unhappy with the way things are that we'll do *anything* to see a change.

> **HAVE A BIG ENOUGH REASON TO BREAK OUT AND TAKE ACTION**

And at that point, all the nicey-nice motivational rah-rah speaking in the world won't do a damn bit of good unless it's backed up with a solid ass kicking. Because while nicey-nice inspiration works for a while, the Normalcy Trap remains, and you're back to where you were to begin with.

Society has taught us all that there are other ways we can just have ideas, avoid taking action, and still "feel" successful... for a short while. Here's what society has taught us that success should look like:

⇨ Being healthy (Just what does that *mean*, anyway?)

⇨ Having all your needs met (What *are* your needs?)

⇨ Paying cash for large items (car, house, kids' college education)

⇨ Love and passion for what you do

⇨ Changing others' lives (What others? How many others?)

These definitions of success sound good... at first. They're not exactly what I'd call specific, and nor do they have any sort of goal measurement that would have an impact on your bottom line (we'll talk about this more in Chapter 11). Most of these definitions of success are what I like to call "feel-good cop-out ideas." Why would I call all these "good" things cop-outs for real success? Because they're not nearly specific enough to give any sort of solid definition of success. I also believe that people who don't feel they can achieve financial riches have convinced themselves they're happy doing without, thus making an excuse for not achieving their true financial dreams and goals and remaining a slave to the Normalcy Trap. It's a way for them to feel good about not being the financial success they *really* want to be, to be "normal," and still to have warm, fuzzy feelings about it. And usually that's because they believe the lie society has thrust down their throats since they were kids... "you can't have *both* happiness *and* money."

Your Choice...

I'll let you in on a little secret... You *can* have both. You *can* escape the Normalcy Trap. Most people just don't believe that because they haven't seen it for themselves or they're not willing to take the action it requires. I think it's high time *you* experienced it for yourself! Happiness has a lot to do with being successful. And so does being stress-free about money. Can you pay cash for large purchases if you're not financially stable or successful? What about the ability to live debt free? How would it feel to pay someone $10,000 and not give it a second thought? What does "success" look like to you? One of the items on that list on the previous page? And if so, let's get harshly honest... Are you using *that* definition of your own success as a cop-out for not thinking and dreaming big enough? Or for remaining a slave to the Normalcy Trap?

As my husband Tony once told me when I was struggling with what could be possible vs. making it reality, "It's *much* easier to believe in the possibility of something rather than in the reality of it, because there is no built-in accountability to what's possible." You can dream all you like, have many ideas, take notes, keep sketchbooks full of mind maps for projects, and work your 9-5 day job hoping *someday* you'll get your big break. *Or*, you can believe in the *reality* of your dream, that it's actually there waiting for you to take hold of it, and finally feel the pressure (and joy) to accomplish those goals that will *make* your dream become reality.

That choice is yours.

> # UNTIL YOU TAKE ACTION ON YOUR DREAM, ALL THE TIME AND MONEY YOU INVEST IN IT IS WORTHLESS

I'm going to throw down a challenge to you right now. Because until you take *action* on your dream, *everything* you invest in toward that dream is *worthless*. It takes consistent, deliberate action to stay away from the Normalcy Trap. If it's important enough to you, you'll find a way. Otherwise, you'll find an excuse. Let's take my physical condition as an example. Right now at this point in my life, opening my dream toy store is more important to me than staying in shape. Eating whatever I can get my hands on out of convenience for my "lack of time" is more important to me than the preparation and planning necessary to eat healthier. While I kept telling myself, "When the store is open and on a regular schedule, I'll create a routine that fits in my workouts and healthy eating," that's only a partial truth. I'm calling bullshit on myself. Because if it *was* important enough to me to take action on it, I'd *make* the time to make it happen and set a new normal for my routine! And until it becomes important enough I *won't* make that time. Right now as I write this, some lower back pain and headaches have started to return almost every day. For me, the pain of staying the same has to be greater than the pain of change before I'll make that change. As I told my husband the other day, "I know what I need to do. I know how to do it. I'm just not willing to do it yet." And *that* is the difference between a successful entrepreneur and an ideologist. Good or bad, the successful *own their own bullshit.*

Most of us live our lives knowing what we need to do, or at least knowing the next step. And usually we know who can help us get to where we want to be. We're just not willing to do the work, take the time, take action, or to suck it up and call bullshit on ourselves in a big enough way that motivates us to *do* it. We're so comfortable sitting in our tiny little box of normalcy, we've built the trap around ourselves and we don't want to peek out to see the brightness of our potential success. So now it's time to make the choice. Do you want to stay on this cop-out "feel-good-for-a-while" path toward success? Or are you ready to actually take that step into the unknown and *be successful?*

Enough excuses... It's time for you to make a commitment *right now* that you're going to make your goals and dreams a priority, break the chains of normalcy, and take that next step of action... before it's too late or the current path becomes so painful you're *forced* to make that change. Let's start with owning your bullshit. Know what you have, know who you are, and take that knowledge and newfound freedom from the Normalcy Trap to the bank!

2

Wantrepreneurs Anonymous

Disclaimer: I watch a lot of *Shark Tank*. As often happens on the show, in one particular episode I recently watched, someone with a very cool-looking product started his pitch to the sharks. At first it sounded good. A great, high-end product, a lot of research, and a very pretty video were all presented.

And then the questions started… the inevitable questions about the money.

"How will we get our investment back?"

"How much of your own money have you invested to date?"

And the other questions about his business like, *"How many have you sold?"*

And… *"How long have you been at this?"*

What's interesting is the lack of answers the "entrepreneur" had to give. He had no actual sales of the product, said he'd been working on it for 10 years, had invested about $130,000 of his own money into it, and had a *failed* Kickstarter campaign, which he quickly blamed on Kickstarter's rules. It was obvious the guy was full of great ideas, lofty unrealistic goals, zero business sense, and most of all, the poison of blame. His Normalcy Trap was the blame game and he was a master at redirecting the sharks' questions and hiding real answers.

But the sharks being experts saw right through his shenanigans.

At one point Mark Cuban said, "**You're not an entrepreneur, you're a *want*repreneur.** Know that and *own* who you are." The guy took huge offense at Mark, but Mark didn't mean it in a condescending way. Mark and the other sharks know there are two types of people who try their hands at business: idea generators and action takers. Idea generators constantly come up with great ideas and grand plans, and while some are able to see a project through to completion, they often discover the need to partner with action takers to bring their ideas into fruition. Action takers can come up with their own ideas as well, and when they do they *immediately implement them,* quickly see results, and rinse and repeat what works. Often action takers come up with fewer ideas than idea generators, and their ideas more often see the light of day due to their swift implementation... unless the idea generators have teams of action takers behind them.

The bottom line is that until they learn how to take action, idea generators are more likely to be *want*repreneurs. They may want all the success they see entrepreneurs enjoy. They may want the massive book sales, the promotions to go without a hitch, the business empire their competitors have built around their products and services, but when it comes time to sit down and actually *do* the work themselves, to push through the tech issues when a promotion flops, to think strategically about their books as a business rather than just an "I like to write" mentality, that's when they halt. Because their line of normalcy is staying in Idea Generator Land; taking action is uncomfortable change to them! That's when they get stuck in the Normalcy Trap. And that's why a project they started 15 years ago is still gathering virtual dust on their external hard drive today.

It's OK if You're a Wantrepreneur... Just Own Who You Are!

The fact is we *need* idea generators. Action takers don't always act on their own ideas; often they run with the ideas of others. Action takers also tend to get so caught up in the process that they also get stuck due to a lack of new problem-solving ideas—*their* Normalcy Trap! Idea generators and action takers can live in symbiotic harmony... if they recognize which type they are, embrace it, own it, and learn to work with the other type to see their mutual dreams come true.

The point that Mark was trying to make was that if you find yourself feeling like a wantrepreneur, you're not a failure. You're just an idea generator who needs to find

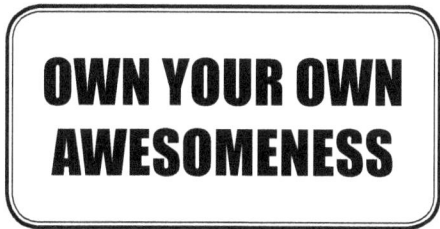

OWN YOUR OWN AWESOMENESS

another way to get your ideas to market, probably by partnering with an action taker. And the wantrepreneur on *Shark Tank* totally missed that memo. In the mini interview after his segment, he was all flustered and angrily said, "I can't believe them. They don't understand the product or my mission. All they cared about was the money."

The fact is they saw he wasn't willing to budge on some of his "ideas" to take action and to reach the level of success they knew the product was capable of reaching. To be successful, idea generators need to be flexible on ways their ideas can manifest into reality and action takers need to remain open to new ideas on which to take action. And wantrepreneurs? Just need to own how awesome they are in where they're currently residing as (usually) idea generators. *And* they should remain open to the process of what it takes to become a full-fledged entrepreneur... *if* that's something they really want for themselves. Idea generators can be successful entrepreneurs if they take responsibility for their ideas and either pass the implementation on to action takers who love to implement others' ideas or partner with someone to hold them accountable to make their ideas reality themselves. The key is knowing the difference and *making a decision* as to what role you want for your business life: *want*repreneur or entrepreneur.

Let me tell you a story about Ginnie. First of all know this: Ginnie was freaking awesome. She worked for my company for several years. I saw her grow, stumble, get distracted, and soar to new heights. I watched as she finally started to figure out what she really wanted and how she fought the deepest desire of her heart. Ginnie acted like an employee. She wanted a steady "retainer" every week for her work. She didn't want to take on other clients besides me. Basically, Ginnie wanted a steady paycheck... and I was willing to give it to her.

Then things started to change. Ginnie began to resent the unrest that accompanies entrepreneurship. She started asking to do other tasks that she didn't really want to do, just for an increase in pay. And then she began to resent her work, our customers, and started to self-sabotage her place in my company. Finally, she had enough and did something drastic. She wrote me a lengthy email demanding things that I was unwilling to give. In our conversation that followed, I matter-of-factly pointed out how she'd sabotaged her role in my business many times, how she kept changing her mind because she couldn't accept what she *really* wanted, and how no employee would act the way she was acting and keep his or her job beyond one day of such behavior.

She was *furious!* "How could you let me go? Why won't you renegotiate... again? Why is this happening to me?" were all questions she asked on our final call together. The fact is Ginnie was a *want*repreneur. She *wanted* the life I had, the freedom she saw, the benefits of the money in my bank account... but she didn't want to do what it takes to get where I am today. My husband often talks about "paying your dues" in business and Ginnie wanted the reward without the payment. It was too scary for her to face the truth of what it really takes to be a successful entrepreneur, so she let her fear get in the way and found an illegitimate way to get what she really wanted; a regular job with a steady paycheck.

The danger of being a wantrepreneur is being so attached to your own ideas that you won't accept advice from others, specifically action takers, who have proven they know what they're talking about. It's in being so focused on your own desires for your project that you ignore the advice of your editor, your coach, etc. It's in not being open to the Upper and Lower Realms of advice and gentle (as well as not-so-gentle) ass kicking coming your way. The biggest danger of all is being so *attached* to your own thoughts and ideas that you push through life with blinders on and blame everyone around you when you stumble, fail, or get stuck.

And attachment to your ideas *always* brings failure... death to something in favor of something else (wanted or unwanted). Every. Single. Time.

In the case of Ginnie, she ended up facing a tough decision. To carry on with her business and get new clients, which she attempted to do at first, or to face her deep-down desire and recognize that just because she was a wantrepreneur it did *not* define her as a failure in life. About a week after my conversation with her and her subsequent firing, I received another email. The subject line read, "You were right." She spent a lot of time dedicated to self-exploration and asking what she really wanted. She told me she was mad that we had said "no employee would act like this," because her angry response was, "I am NOT an employee!" In hindsight she realized that's what she actually *wanted* to be. And her Normalcy Trap was constantly bringing her back to her chief desire: a steady paycheck with the "security" of a "real job."

A war was going on within her as she discovered what she really wanted was not to be an entrepreneur or even a wantrepreneur, but to work for a visionary organization and support it in the role of an employee. Once she came to that realization, she landed a new position at a company in her town that fit every qualification she was looking for.

Going from Want to Ent...

If after reading this you still want to press on to be a successful *ent*repreneur, the best way to accomplish this weighty task is to turn your *want* into "*ent*" and to become a full-fledged, driven, passionate entrepreneur. To *want* it badly enough that you do what it takes to *learn* the skills necessary to turn your ideas into action. This achievement is entirely possible for idea generators as long as they identify and avoid their Normalcy Trap. The want is great—you need to want what you're doing in order to have the passion and drive to get through inevitable difficulties and road blocks. And when you combine that with the *action*—the primary characteristic of a successful *ent*repreneur—you'll see a significant difference in your growth, your product sales, the reach of your message, and ultimately your bank account.

WANT YOUR DREAM BADLY ENOUGH TO DO WHAT IT TAKES TO GET IT

To go from "want" to "ent" takes what I call the Five Knows, the first being know your **market**. On an episode of *Shark Tank* a wantrepreneur was pitching a towel for beachgoers. The problem was the product looked like *and* was packaged and sold as if it were a woman's wrap, not a towel, but their marketing tactics promoted it as a towel. The wantrepreneur couldn't figure out why sales were low, yet the packaging was confusing customers who couldn't figure out if it was a towel or a wrap. If you're selling a product or service, you have to know your market. What is it they're looking for? What problem do they want solved? What pain do they want relieved? In the towel vs. wrap example, these wantrepreneurs could cater to either market with just a simple change in packaging and marketing. They had a great idea and by partnering with an action taker (whether a Shark or someone else), they would be able to target the market better, sell a lot more product, and generate enough income to have a viable company.

Almost every business book I've ever read has a section in it about knowing your market. What they don't seem to touch on is that idea generators have so many ideas coming at them from all directions all the time that they hardly think about their market. And the typical action taker is head-down action taking so much they don't take the time to know the market either. Yet this is one of the foundational requirements to be a successful entrepreneur. If you don't know who would benefit from your product or service and *how* they would benefit, you have no leg to stand on to try to sell it to them once it's completed!

The second know is know your **competition**. What gives *you* the edge in your market? Here's a news flash for you… *nothing* is new. Everything has already been done before. You may have come up with an idea that combines some other ideas into something "new" or think you've just come up with something truly innovative, but if you follow your thought processes along to when you first got the idea, it came from somewhere. A seed was sown that grew into a thought, then an idea, and if you take action on it, it may be considered truly innovative… yet there is probably still someone else in the world who has done something similar. The key to tapping into success as an entrepreneur in your market is to know who your competitors are, what they're doing, and how *your* product or service is better.

When I taught authors how to know their competition I told them to research other books in their genre that targeted their same audience, then read all the negative reviews. What were reviewers complaining about? What did they wish was actually in the book? What steps did they want to be made clearer? By filling these gaps in their own books my authors were able to have higher quality books than their competition, and often they outsold those competitors' books. This "fill the gap" strategy works for any product or service in any industry or niche. Take time to do your research before putting out any new product or service and be mindful of the time you allot to this task, as idea generators often get "better" ideas as they research and action takers typically take so much action thoroughly researching that they neglect actually creating the product or service.

Know your **numbers...** Income *and* outgo! Numbers don't lie and nothing says whether you're successful or not more clearly than your numbers. While you don't have to know the exact dollar amount your company makes, it's essential that you know the bulk of what's coming in (gross sales) as well as what's going out (expenses, purchases, etc.). If you don't have your personal finances in order you'll be flying blind in your business. Billion Dollar Buyer host and venture capitalist Tilman Fertitta said it best, "I ask people what they do in sales, how much money they made last year, what their cost of sales is, and they don't even know. If you don't know your numbers, you're going out of business. I don't care how good your product is."

Knowing your numbers doesn't have to be complicated. I recommend you try out a program like Mint.com or Mvelopes.com to start putting together a budget (both personal and business). I can't tell you how many times I've procrastinated on running the company budgets for my businesses only to breathe a sigh of relief once it's done, because in this instance knowledge really *is* power! Flying blind to where your money is going or how you're making it is not the epitome of "ignorance is bliss." In the case of money, ignorance is simply the first step in a long path toward anxiety, stress, and ulcers. Knowledge really is power when it comes to your numbers. Knowledge lets you know when you have a surplus in one category, like association memberships, and can move that money to another category in need, like inventory. This knowledge also lets you discover where "tiny" expenses such as office supplies could be bleeding your company dry.

The bottom line is, if you want to keep moving forward with blinders on toward your numbers, you'll never have the deep breath of relief that everything is covered and you'll put yourself under significant amounts of undue stress. As soon as you sit down and take the time to tally up *all* your expenses and allot your income in proper percentages where it needs to go to cover those expenses, *then* you will see that things are better than you thought they were and you may even discover a surplus you didn't realize you had!

TAKE TIME TO KNOW YOUR NUMBERS AND EARN PEACE OF MIND

Know your **limits**. Did you know that anxiety disorders are the most common mental illness in the United States, affecting 40 million adults aged 18 and older? That's about 18% of the population *every year*! And nearly half the people diagnosed with an anxiety disorder are also diagnosed with depression. Having fought depression and anxiety disorders myself and having had close relatives and friends who struggle with it, I firmly believe that both these disorders are precursors to burnout. Anxiety is a warning sign that something isn't right. Whether it's a chemical imbalance or mental fatigue, the fact is the more you push yourself to succeed and the more you push to get that one project done (the one you don't really *want* to do, but feel you *should* do), the faster you will burn out.

A few months before I started writing this book I noticed a change in my body. I started fighting chronic fatigue again. All I wanted to do was sleep. It could be a beautiful day outside and I just wanted to disappear. I had no passion for work and I beat myself up for not wanting to work. I started "shoulding" all over myself as I said things to myself like, "You should know better than to push so hard" and "You should *want* to finish that project; what's wrong with you?" This pattern of "shoulding" led me down a nasty rabbit hole full of distracting brambles.

It took a coaching call from someone in my Upper Realm (read more about this realm in Chapter 5) to pull me out of it. She snapped me back to reality by having me list out all the "things" I'd "done" or "accomplished" in the past 30 days. It was a *lot* of "stuff" and I put all those words in quotes because the sense of accomplishment

CHALLENGE YOURSELF TO SPEND AT LEAST ONE FULL DAY UNTETHERED FROM YOUR PHONE

I got from doing all the "things" was a false emotion. It wasn't anything that actually benefited me; rather, I felt I wasn't good enough because I didn't do *more*. And most of what I'd been doing was what other people wanted me to do. I found myself tied to my phone and computer and resenting any time I got an email or private message from *anybody*, even my husband. It got to the point where I'd glare at that screen lighting up and say out loud, "Who wants a piece of me NOW?!" To say I was miserable is an understatement.

And here's the kicker... once I recognized the resentment for what it was—burnout—I honestly thought it would take me months to recover. Part of me didn't want to even try because I'd gotten used to this being my normal. I was caught in my own personal Normalcy Trap. My Upper Realm coach challenged me to spend one day away from my phone. One day untethered from the wants and desires of other people. One day to do whatever the hell I wanted.

I paused. I struggled.

I suddenly realized *I* was addicted to the *"need"* others had of me. I needed to be needed. I saw my value in others' desire for a piece of my time. So in a sense I was resenting my own resentment!

In that moment I had power because I realized I had a choice. I could *choose* to keep being all things to all people. Or I could *choose* to take a break. I chose the break. I spent one day in my art studio with music blaring, playing with new mediums and new techniques. The first piece I created was made out of a lot of anger. In fact I wrote the words "Angry" and "HATE!" on the canvas before covering them up with melted wax and all sorts of other things. As I created I realized just how resentful of my own choices I had become. And that's the key right there—I was resentful of MY OWN choices. Not someone else's. I couldn't blame any of my emotional spiral on anyone else. It was *my* choice to constantly be at the beck and call of my customers, friends, family, and even acquaintances I hardly knew.

That day I left my phone in the house so even my husband had to walk out to the studio to talk to me. And I felt so refreshed by the end of the day that I decided to repeat the process the next day. And you know what? What I thought would take me weeks or even months to feel, I felt within two *days.* It felt like my brain had completely rebooted. My body had reset. My energy reserves were filled. And suddenly I was full of love for my work again.

It reminded me how easy it is to get caught up in what others want from us and how we humans *need* to recharge on a regular basis. Now I try to make "technology-free me time" in my studio at least once a month because it really is that important. Any time I feel the dreariness and anxiety of burnout approaching I put myself in timeout and send my body and mind off to the studio. Every time I go kicking and screaming. And every time within 15 minutes of burying myself in the art I love so much, I feel refreshed and re-energized. And I wonder yet again why I don't make more time for this.

Know the feelings in your body when you're approaching burnout. They may be anxiety, depression, illness… and that might be your Normalcy Trap like it was for me. Take time for something you know recharges you and do it without any technology around. Try it for one hour, then one day, then two days. Before you know it you'll be making this activity a part of your normal routine, setting the bar for what's "normal" for you a little higher, avoiding your old Normalcy Trap!

The fifth know is… **know that you *don't know squat.*** The most dangerous mental place to be is in a state of, "I already know all that. I got this. I don't need it as much as they do." One of our employees started training session with his peers and said those things about the training. The training was meant to be for personal development and team building in a setting in which everyone could learn from each other and work better together. But this person bailed out early because he "didn't need it." What's ironically funny is that my husband and I recognized exactly where his mindset was as we both went through the same training at a much older age with a lot more experience and already making a shit ton more money than he's ever seen in his life. Going back to the third know, "know your numbers," the fact is that if he already knew everything there was to learn in that training session it would be reflected in his bank account. He'd be such a huge success oozing in so much cash, he wouldn't need a job, much less *want* to work for us.

Coming to grips with the fact that you don't know squat is anything but comfortable. The voices in your Normalcy Trap will tell you that you already know it, you can skip that part, you don't need to invest in a coach, etc. And that's because those voices are trying to protect

ALWAYS BE WILLING TO LEARN

you from the one thing they fear most—*change*. And yet if you ignored those voices and pushed yourself out of your Normalcy Trap into the light of the truth that you don't know squat, you'll *know* more. You'll *know* that anything is possible. That there's always more to learn. Which takes me to my last bit of advice for this chapter: Always be willing to learn. Learn from yourself, from peers, from your coaches and mentors, others you admire, and also from anyone who works for you. Until you learn to play in all three realms of Asskickonomics® simultaneously, you will constantly hit the same old brick walls in your business. Once you recognize that you *don't* know it all, you'll grow into and experience the success you desire.

3

What IS Success Anyway?

Successful entrepreneurs know that having a success-focused mindset is the essential foundation of every idea they want to breathe into reality. This mindset is what creates millionaires, and *all* millionaires are successful in spite of themselves. They're human just like you. They make mistakes—a *lot* of mistakes. But what sets them apart from the unsuccessful is the fact that they're willing to do the work, learn, and get their asses kicked in the process. Lori Greiner from *Shark Tank* describes it this way, "A brilliant idea doesn't guarantee success. Real magic comes from a brilliant idea combined with willpower, tenacity, and a willingness to make mistakes."

Successful entrepreneurs know their shit, from their bottom-line numbers to how much time they can set aside for family and vacations, *and* they keep an open mind in all three realms of Asskickonomics which we will cover more in-depth later. The "secret" to their success is that *there is no secret*. They understand there's no such thing as "overnight" success. Success is something you see, want, and pursue no matter the cost. You have to *want* it bad enough to get it. It's not handed to anyone on a silver platter. Truly successful entrepreneurs do what needs to be done behind closed doors when no one else is watching. They pay their dues, often working late and rising early, to become the best they can be in their chosen field. They make thousands of mistakes, get back up... and do it all over again no matter how painful making those mistakes may be. Another powerful *Shark*, Barbara Corcoran said, "If you're competitive and pigheaded enough to get over failures without wasting time feeling sorry for yourself, and if you can inspire enough good people to join you, you can pretty much become as rich as you want."

So why are there not more successful millionaire business owners? Why is it most people in business seem to get by with just the bare basics to keep their doors open and feed their families?

The Three Biggest "Reasons" Why You're Not Successful

Let's cut to the chase. I put "reasons" in quotes because I honestly believe these are *not* legitimate reasons for not meeting your goals... yet they're the reasons most often given by my students and fellow entrepreneurs. Chances are you've used these reasons yourself. (From now on I'll call them what they are—*excuses*.)

"I don't have the time."

BULLSHIT. You have the *same* amount of time in a day as everyone else. That's 86,400 seconds every day, to be exact. It takes only one second to say, "Thank you." That's over 86,000 opportunities you have to give thanks in any day. You get 168 hours every week. If you only work on your goals for one hour per week, that's pocket change when it comes to time and eventually you'll complete that goal. It's all about perspective. If you audit your time for a week, you'll clearly see your priorities and how many times interruptions set you off course. Is it your priority to taxi your kids to a dozen extracurricular events every month? To cook at home instead of eating fast food? Or is it your priority to make sure you don't miss that next sitcom or favorite TV show? Or to spend hours at high-end restaurants being waited on?

It doesn't matter *what* your priorities are. What matters is that you know what they are, you're OK with them, and you recognize you have the choice to set them, eliminating the "I don't have the time" excuse.

The fact is we humans waste precious minutes every day... minutes that add up to hours that could be invested in our goals. Most goals can be worked on in bite-sized pieces from just about anywhere. When I take my car into the shop, even for a quick 10-minute oil change, I know

RECOGNIZE YOUR EXCUSES FOR WHAT THEY ARE—EXCUSES

that's 10 minutes I have to do something constructive. I always have my iPad on me, and if it's going to be a longer appointment I make sure to bring my computer. And just in case the shop's Wi-Fi is down, I carry a MiFi card. It's all about *preparation* and *motivation*. The fact is *everyone* makes time for what's important to them. **Everyone**. Family, eating at home, working on projects—these are all things that are important to me, so I make time for them. And if I get sick and *really* want to binge watch a show on Netflix? You can bet I have my iPad or my computer with me and I'm plugging away at something instead of just melting my body into the couch for hours on end. It's definitely not the most productive way to get shit done, but *some* progress is definitely better than *no* progress!

"I don't have the money."

While you may have limited resources, I've also found the same rule applied to time applies here as well. People *always* find a way to get the money for something they *really* want. Whether it's by picking up a second job, working overtime, starting a business, getting a loan, asking family or friends for help… if they want it bad enough they *will find a way.* Just go to a trailer park and walk into the one that has the car out front with pimped out wheels and a badass stereo system. They probably have a big screen TV and other tech toys inside as well, yet they're so broke they can't afford rent at a nicer place. And often the "poor" people who complain about never having enough money squander it away on eating out at fancy restaurants and buying shit they don't need like cigarettes and tattoos when they *do* have a surplus. (Tough wakeup call: What did you spend your tax refund on?)

IF YOUR GOAL IS IMPORTANT ENOUGH TO YOU, YOU WILL FIND A WAY TO ACHIEVE IT

In his book *Shut Up, Stop Whining, and Get a Life*, financial "un-guru" Larry Winget says, "A prosperity consciousness is based on your belief that there is more than enough for you and everyone else to be secure in all areas of life. All you have to do is be willing to do whatever it takes in order to make it happen." If your goal is important enough to you, you'll find a way to earn the money to invest in the resources you need to make it happen. Until it's that important to you, you won't. It's that simple.

"I don't have the energy."

You may be on disability. You may have a chronic illness. And having lived most of my life with chronic illness, I can understand. However, this is just an excuse—a story that you're living in so you don't have to take responsibility to face what's actually holding you back. It may be fear of success (what if it grows too fast and

I can't keep up?) or fear of failure (what will people think of me if I can't make it work?). Either way, you can't use the "I don't have energy" excuse not to take action on your goals because I've watched a paraplegic woman type an entire 250-page book out on her computer using a pencil in her mouth to touch the keys.

So who cares if you don't have the energy? What about being thankful for the energy you *do* have and using it wisely? As Zig Ziglar said, "The more you are thankful for what you have, the more you will have to be thankful for." Want more energy? Start practicing gratitude for the energy you have and watch as you gain more. Be thankful for the increase and it will increase again. Before you know it, you'll have the strength and drive to get your next project done. Again, if your goal is important enough to you, you'll *find* the energy to make it happen!

Measure Your Success

There are many ways entrepreneurs can measure their success. It can be the number of written goals they reach in a day, week, month, or year. It can be as specific as the number of products they sold in a month. Some entrepreneurs measure their personal success by the amount of money in their bank accounts, figuring net and gross sales (gross always sounds better... and it's less accurate) or the number of books they read each week. And others prefer to measure it in the more ambiguous, harder-to-determine analysis of time for freedom to do what they want, when they want, and where they want, including taking time for their hobbies, travel, family activities, etc.

What's important is not exactly what you choose to measure, but that you have some sort of gauge to measure your own success that works for you. It needs to be something specific that you can compare each week, month, and year to the previous weeks, months, and years. Measuring your success doesn't have to be hard. I have several measurements that I personally use to see if I've reached my previous months' goals. The most telling one for me is my gross income (because again, gross income always looks better and it's more motivating for me). I keep a sticky note on the wall beside my computer and on it I write a tally of my gross business income for every month. Next to that is a sticky note for the next year, and the next, with room for a fourth year. Every year I can easily and directly compare the previous months' numbers to this year's current month. For me the most important thing to know in my business is the *numbers*. While I do measure other activities to watch my progress in other areas, the numbers are my bottom-line assessment of whether I need to make changes the next month.

Of all the things you may choose to measure, numbers don't lie. So whatever you choose to measure your success, make sure one of those choices includes numbers. Because while having time to be your kids' taxi service to a dozen extra curricular activities every week might be your idea of being successful, having that time means nothing if you're still struggling to pay your electric bill.

> ## OF ALL THE THINGS YOU CHOOSE TO MEASURE, YOUR NUMBERS WON'T LIE

The Five Basic Success "Secrets"

You've probably heard many "secrets" to success. Chances are you're a success book junkie and own more than a half-dozen books on the topic, each outlining a dozen or more success secrets. The fact is there's no *one* secret to success. There are five. OK, I'm just kidding... but really, there are five success strategies that I focus on more than all the others I've heard over the years.

Success Strategy #1: The Power of Simplicity

Unless you've been living in a hole your entire business life, you've probably heard the phrase, "Keep it simple." Even if you've heard this phrase before and think you have it handled, I encourage you to keep reading... I *guarantee* you're not living fully into the power of simplicity!

It is so incredibly easy to overcomplicate anything, from your business card design to troubleshooting stressful situations. The phenomenon of over-complication is easily noticeable in graphic design students. It seems like coming up with a simple design should be easy, yet not one single student I've ever encountered has been able to master simplicity in design at the first try. Newbies always overcomplicate their early designs. And then they often get stuck in a "style" of overcomplicating before something snaps into place and they figure it out. It's that magical on/off switch in the brain that cannot be taught. Either you learn how to look at your world and simplify everything or you continue to find yourself stuck in the cycle of overcomplication.

One thing that can help to flip that switch from complicated to simple is to recognize what overcomplicating everything is costing you. Because unlike the power of simplicity, complication costs you something. Either you spend more time on a project trying to "fix" everything and make it perfect or you keep throwing money at a situation hoping it resolves itself in the quickest (albeit not always the simplest) way possible. Unless you learn how to simplify your to-dos, projects, branding, business, and life, you'll find yourself devoting a *lot* more energy than necessary and hitting burnout over and over again with fewer breaks in between burnout strikes. Overcomplicating can also cost you relationships as you become stressed, strained, and burn the candle not only at both ends, but straight down the middle.

In short, overcomplicating can be distilled down to *one* thing: making shit hard. The more you overcomplicate something, the harder it is. The more you overcomplicate your business, your processes, and your life, the more stressed out you will be. And this stress has a direct impact on your success.

Think about the last time you found yourself making something hard. Or maybe it's easier to recall a time you were dealing with an agency that was overcomplicating an issue... like a bank, a law firm, or the IRS. You may have said to yourself, "There *has* to be an easier way!" Any time you notice overcomplication happening, take a step back. Take a deep breath and ask yourself, "How can I make this simpler?" The more you become aware of when you're making shit hard, the more you'll be equipped to simplify matters before they get out of hand and cost you something you value.

Success Strategy #2: The Comparison Game

This is a trap most entrepreneurs fall into at least once or twice. Some even have a zip code in Comparisonland. There are many times when even I feel like I will never measure up to anyone in my industry, so there's no reason I should do what I do.

A friend and I recently had a conversation about him getting into the world of online training. I asked him what was holding him back from taking the plunge into what's been one of my most successful endeavors in business and he said, "Somebody else out there already knows this topic better than I do and is therefore better suited to teach it." He fell into the most common trap of comparing himself to others... people he doesn't even know! I asked him if he thought there was someone better qualified to teach about book publishing than I am. He said he couldn't say, since he didn't know my industry that well. I laughed... then laughed some more. Perplexed, he just looked at me. I was literally wiping tears from my eyes from laughing so hard, then told him, "There's *always* going to be someone better at it than you. *Always*. Someone is always striving to beat the last person's record. Whether in sports or business or writing, the fact is if you know more than someone else who wants to learn, you're qualified to get your message out to them in whatever way possible, inspire them, and help them to take action. There are people in the world that will only listen to the way you can deliver a message. And those others who know more than you? Well they're not the people you're trying to reach anyway." At the end of our conversation he was still confused because he's so stuck in the comparison game. He couldn't figure out how to break free or that his message was indeed valuable.

The comparison game is dangerous because it's very easy to get stuck in a continuous loop and to end up frustrated at both the fact you can't finish what you start and the stark reality that whether you finish it or not, someone, somewhere out there could probably do a better job than you. The only way out of this loop is to recognize that first, you don't know others' full

> # THE MOST DANGEROUS GAME YOU CAN PLAY IS THE COMPARISON GAME

stories, where they come from, what they've gone through, etc. You have no right to judge how awesome they are in comparison to you because you don't know what they've done or what they've sacrificed to get where they are. And you're refusing to look at what *you* have done and sacrificed to get where *you* are! After it sinks in that you don't know their full story and therefore you have no foundation with which to compare yourself to them, it's time for you to set the most important comparison...

> ## ONLY COMPARE YOURSELF TO YOUR OWN GOALS

Compare yourself to your *own* goals. Past, present, and future, you have the ability to set yourself up for success by striving to beat your previous goals every single time. This task is easier said than done and it's a habit that will serve you well in any endeavor you wish to pursue.

Now it's time for you to face the stark reality that the reason you keep comparing yourself to others and *not* taking action is actually because *you don't want to*. Do you really want that cup of coffee at the local coffee shop, but it's pouring down outside so you either run as fast as you can or hunt for an umbrella? If you want it bad enough, you'll find a way to get it. And that's true of any goal, dream, wish, or desire. Want it? Go get it. The only thing stopping you is yourself.

Success Strategy #3: The Realistic Goal

We'll be covering this a lot more in-depth in Chapter 11 so I'm going to keep this section short and let you flip over there for more detail. You've probably heard of SMART goals. While there are variations on the theme, the most commonly accepted definition of a SMART goal is specific, measurable, attainable, realistic, and time-bound. I'll definitely mention those again later, so for now I want to focus on what I believe to be the most important element of SMART: realistic.

Resolutions almost always fail because they're not realistic. They may be specific, measurable, and have a deadline, and you may *think* they're attainable... but how many times have you said, "THIS is my year to lose 100 pounds!" Or, "This year I'm going to read three new books every month!" Unless you get surgery, speed read, or take time to listen to audio books, none of these is realistic. It's much more practical to have *one* realistic "I've arrived" goal with many (sometimes hundreds) of small in-between goals, starting with something very simple you can complete in the next 30 days.

For example, when I started working with a personal trainer right before Christmas with the goal to lose weight, get in shape, and straighten my crooked knees, I set small, achievable, realistic goals and hit almost every one of them. I lost 30 lbs, my knees did indeed get straight, and I got stronger. Then I got the bright idea to open a new business and all the stress and lack-of-time-excuses that came along with it sabotaged my fitness goals... because they were no longer realistic to my current situation. I gained the weight back because convenience became more realistic with my busier-than-usual lifestyle.

This is why I recommend that you have many "little" goals along the way to your big goal. Those small goals must be adaptable to change, otherwise you'll never meet, exceed, or stick to your "I've arrived" goal after you reach it. Since starting that business my workout routine has pretty much gone to hell, my sugar and convenience food intake skyrocketed, I've gained back over 20lbs, and overall, I have less energy and strength.

Was it the personal trainer's fault? Were my goals too big? No. The problem is I pressured myself to stick to my "I've arrived" goal when life got impractical... without a little-goals-to-stay-there game plan. Just this week I've started back to the mini goals. Lessen my sugar intake. Stop snacking late at night. Get down to my dojo workout room and just *stand* in it. Because once I'm standing in it, at bare minimum I'll end up stretching, hitting the bag, and at some point, work myself back into doing an entire workout routine. It will take these little tiny baby step goals to get back to my "I've arrived" goal.

Take a moment to write down your "I've arrived" goal. It's OK if you have to think about it first; just make it a point to write it down within the next 24 hours. Then underneath that goal write one tiny little thing you can do within the next 30 days to get closer to achieving that goal. (Hint: Grab *Asskickonomics: The Workbook* and do these exercises while you're reading this book.) Work on that tiny little thing, then the next tiny little thing, then the next… and watch your big goal come closer to completion with each passing day!

Success Strategy #4: The Power of YOUR Project

There are millions of copycats in the world. In one of my businesses, the world of digital products and training courses, copycatism runs rampant. I have colleagues whose products regularly get ripped off and sold on black hat sites. Other people in the industry copy ideas and sell them almost word for word like the original, with just barely enough changed to avoid a copyright lawsuit. And sleazebags who over promise and under deliver because all they're doing is copying someone else's hard work that they don't really believe in themselves (they just see a fast path to cash) run amuck in general. For those like me who pour heart and soul of our own ideas and innovations into our projects, it's disheartening to see someone else rip off the idea and run with it. No matter how legal it may be, there's a difference between legal and ethical. And unfortunately most human beings are not innovators, so it's much easier to do what someone else is already doing rather than tap into their own uniqueness.

But here's what those copycatists don't understand. The reason innovators have such a loyal following and have the numbers to back up their success is because they've figured out how to learn from others, then pave their own path. If you want to taste true success, learning from others is a fantastic way to start. However don't do what those others are doing just because you think it's cool or it's been "proven" to make money. Instead, view every idea—every project—in light of *your* unique ideas and goals. Find a way to be different, to spin the idea and make it uniquely yours.

For example, before writing this section this morning I saw a promotion for a journal product. I keep tabs on journal products due to my popular Journal Design Basics training (JournalDesignBasics.com), which was the first of its type

IT'S TIME FOR YOU TO PAVE YOUR OWN PATH

to appear in my industry. Was it the first time someone had trained on creating journals? No. But I took that idea and created my own spin on how to design niche journals and then taught my students how to create a journal from scratch and publish it... in two days. I showed them how to create a template, adapt that same journal to another niche, and publish two journals in two days, which I did live in front of everyone. So when I saw the "journal" promotion, I had to check it out. It turns out that the person creating this new product was not a current student of mine. The only training she'd received from me was my free introductory one. She took the concepts I taught in the free training and turned it into a product of templates that she created to help people adapt and create their own journals even faster.

This is a good example of taking an idea, spinning it, and making it your own. This product creator saw my idea and created something completely new and different from it. And I honestly believe she will be successful because she added her uniqueness to the idea.

Success Strategy #5: The Power of the Positive

If there's any success strategy more powerful than any other, it all comes down to your mindset. Mark Cuban says it best, "It doesn't matter how many times you have failed, you only have to be right once." He sums up what all successful entrepreneurs have discovered—that true success comes from focusing on ways you can succeed, not ways you've failed. This most influential success strategy requires only one thing... positive thinking. In fact while all the other strategies in this chapter are great, without a positive mindset all the work in the world won't make you successful. This mindset is the most powerful profit-boosting truth you'll ever need. And implementing it can be easier said than done!

BE AWARE OF HOW MANY TIMES YOU SPEAK POSITIVELY OR NEGATIVELY

It all comes down to awareness and using that awareness to set boundaries with your mind. For example, until it was pointed out to me how many times I said, "I can't afford," I didn't realize how much I said it. "Can't" is a negative word that causes the opposite reaction in your world than its positive counterpart. In that moment when I became aware of just how many times I said this negative phrase, I made a conscious decision to set a boundary with my speech. It didn't fully change overnight and every time I caught myself saying, "I can't afford" I changed it to, "I choose not to spend" instead. So "I can't afford to go to that movie" became "I choose not to go to that movie right now." The power in changing one simple phrase and creating a *choice* changed my entire outlook. Money started to flow my way. My products were well received. My service business increased to the point I couldn't handle the workload anymore and had to hire help. My entire income shifted as soon as I took the power of positive choice and applied it to my negative thinking, and it continued to grow to a million-dollar business!

Your final assignment from this chapter is to become aware of how many times you say "can't" or another negative word you may frequently repeat. Once you're aware of those words and phrases, ask someone close to you to hold you accountable to change them to positive choice phrases instead. If you have kids, they will *love* this exercise, and it teaches *them* the power of positivity as well!

Applying the power of the positive may also require that you let go of relationships with people who no longer help you. Misery attracts negativity and this is extremely true in those you hang out with, including family. Be willing to limit your exposure to people who will encourage your negativity only because they themselves are miserable. If you want to be successful, this is a hard sacrifice you will be asked to make at one point or another. Success in business *requires* positive thinking and that includes the mindsets of those you surround yourself with!

4

Successful Mind Hacks

Mind-hacking your way to success is something all truly successful entrepreneurs understand and explore on a regular basis. At the end of the day it doesn't matter how much money is in your bank account or how many houses you own. If you're miserable, if you worry, and if you place yourself under a ton of stress, you're focusing on the negative and you will attract more of it. It's incredibly easy to see the negative and to hold onto those thoughts. After all, they're comfortable and known, a common Normalcy Trap. But they're slowly poisoning you and sabotaging your success.

Habits, priorities, expectations, planning, clutter, and self-thinking all have roles to play in mind-hacking your way to success. In this chapter we're going to deep-dive into the depths of these roles and exactly how they will make or break your success as an ass-kicking entrepreneur.

The Importance of Habits

Do you have the tendency to think the worst about an unexpected situation? Do you often approach problems that come up with the words "never" or "always"? Do you spend a chunk of your day sitting or sleeping? Do you have more on your to-do list than you'll ever get done in a day? What about waiting until the last minute to do pretty much everything? Or being habitually late? How often do you feel disappointment in people, purchases, etc.?

> # HABITS SET YOU UP FOR FAILURE OR SUCCESS

Habits set you up for failure or success. They can be good, bad, or even ugly. As you start to analyze and pay attention to your habits throughout the day, how you react (or respond) to situations that come up will say a lot about if your habits are healthy or harmful. If you answered "yes" to any of the questions I listed above, you're living a potentially stressful life. I know that because most of those questions came up for me when I started self-analyzing my habits and the role they played in my success (or lack thereof).

I'm going to bare my soul for a moment. I'm extremely hard on myself. Like holding myself to higher standards than any human could ever possibly achieve and if I don't achieve them I'm a horrible person and the entire world hates me kind of hard. My life coach calls it my "van down by the river" syndrome. It's my most common mindset Normalcy Trap and it's a downward spiral to thinking that just because one tiny issue arises, I'm suddenly broke, friendless, and living in a van down by the river. When put in that perspective it seems silly. Yet it happens to me over and over and over and... you get the idea.

This is an issue I struggle with a lot. It comes up several times per month and every time it does I make it worse by telling myself, "I should've known better." I start "shoulding" all over myself, making me feel worse and even more deserving of that van down by the river! This habit-mindset trap costs me time, energy, and often money in poor financial decisions while I'm stuck in this way of thinking (you know shopping releases good endorphins, right?). And this trap is oh-so-difficult to pull myself out of. Usually I have to call on the help of friends to mindset-slap me upside the head to get me to see that it's not as big a deal as I'm making it out to be, and to point out exactly what this trap is costing me.

If you notice you have habits that creep up every time you want to work on your goal project(s), don't push those thoughts aside. Pay extra special close attention to each one and do a mindset audit to see how many times this same thing comes up for you during a month. As you track your habits in this manner, more will be revealed to you. You may think they're good, as you're getting something out of them, and that's OK. If the habit serves you in a positive way, keep it! Once you start to track your habits there are practical things you can do to mind-hack your way out of those habit-mindset traps and make the leap to habitual success. Some are physical, some mental, and all are life- and business-changing, so let's go in-depth on these success mind hacks now.

You've Heard It Before... Prioritize!

You've probably heard all sorts of methods to prioritize your day. Make a list, mark your top priorities with letters in alphabetical order, so A, B, and C get done first, etc. Schedule your highest priority tasks in your calendar so they get off your to-do list and become an event. Get clear on your goals and make your to-do list match those goals.

There are endless ways to prioritize your life and business tasks. One of my favorites that I use all the time is the calendar method listed above. And I've found another way that seems to work better for more creative, free-flowing, non-conforming types. If I'm feeling especially overwhelmed, I make a to-do list. Then I analyze that list and ask, "Which task is the #1, must-do-TODAY-or-else-I'll-die level of importance?" If none pops out at me (I mean, c'mon, dying *is* a little extreme), I just ask myself which *one* task *must* be done *today*. Then I get off my ass and ***do it!***

> # THERE'S NO SECRET TO BUTT-IN-CHAIR ACTION

There's no secret to butt-in-chair-action; there's no magic. It's simply making the decision to make it happen. *Then* after that #1 task is completed to my satisfaction I look at my to-do list again and ask, "Now, which task do I *feel* like doing?" This question is important because you probably don't feel like doing the #1 most important task, and while you may feel a little better once it's done, your child-brain is crying out for satisfaction to do something it *wants* to do instead. By tapping into your emotions, you're tapping into that child-brain, and by doing that next task you're satisfying your child-brain so it will stop screaming at you for attention and you can tackle the *next* day's #1 priority task.

Keeping a balance of "must do this shit that I hate" and "but I really *want* to do that over there" is important to keep your mind happy. So don't beat yourself up for doing something you *want* to do instead of another task on your list that you *have* to do. Just make sure you use your want-task as a reward for your #1 priority task for that day.

Expect (a Little) Less

Having too high expectations can burn you… big time. Whether you expect too much of yourself or of those around you, chronically high expectations set you up for constant disappointment. Expecting less of someone or a situation doesn't mean you will suddenly turn into the family Eeyore or become the world's biggest pessimist. Usually if you have a habit of setting too high expectations, all expecting less will do is bring you down to a realistic view of how the situation should work out.

For example, have you ever given someone a loan and never been repaid? Then resentment set in and before you knew it the relationship felt strained? You probably expected them to pay you back in a timely manner, which shouldn't be that high an expectation, but unfortunately in this day of chronic human irresponsibility it can be. I learned long ago that if I gave money to anyone, whether *they* said it was a loan or not, I treated it as a gift instead. By not holding the expectation that they would pay me back within a specific timeframe, it didn't affect our relationship at all and I ended up pleasantly surprised if they did.

The secret to building a habit around expecting less is to make it a goal to live in a constant state of being pleasantly surprised. Expect less of yourself and amaze yourself with your results. Expect less of those around you and you'll remove the pressure they may feel to perform or walk on eggshells around you. Expect less of your business results and return on investment and you remove the attachment to how your projects will perform once they're completed, which will dramatically reduce the amount of stress typically associated with launching a new product, service, or program. And you'll soon discover that by expecting less you're removing your attachment to an outcome... and that simple concept *is* the very foundation upon which success is built.

Plan More

I'll be the first to raise my hand: I'm a chronic non-planner. I loathe planning. It annoys the shit out of me. I used to feel like the sole purpose of the agenda planners and daytimers lining office supply store shelves was to mock me. I thrive on the adrenaline that comes from flying by the seat of my pants. So when the first business coach I hired told me to use a planner to plan out my to-dos, my goals, and my appointments, I laughed at him. I remember sitting across the table at Panera Bread from Mack and saying, "Are you KIDDING ME? No. No freaking way." That's how much I *hated* planning. However, Mack got on my case and with a little well-placed guilt manipulation made me promise to head over to Staples as soon as our meeting was over and pick up a planner. Which I did... grunting and complaining the entire way.

That little book changed my life.

Not only did I see an instant change in my stress levels the day I started using it, but I stopped missing appointments, I stopped double-booking myself, and my productivity soared. I was convinced. Maybe planning wasn't such a bad thing after all.

Fast-forward to today and while the tools I use for planning have changed over the years, I still live by my planner. I've also learned a lot more about myself and how I get projects done. The fact is I'm motivated by deadlines. I love procrastination, but not for the aspect of putting off to-dos. I love it because when the deadline is looming the next day it puts a fire under the ass of my productivity and I get more done in much less time than I do if the deadline is a week away. I've had virtual assistants (VAs) who couldn't work with me because of how I kept putting things off until the last minute. I had other people, including well-meaning coaches and well-known speakers, tell me that I was shooting my success in the foot because of my "planning" strategies.

I started to think something was wrong with me. I started to compare myself with other entrepreneurs who had their entire products done and ready to launch a month before their actual launch dates... when I was sitting there scrambling to get my project up before my deadline to promote it... the next day. And it took the advice of one of my team members when I was having a compare-myself-to-everybody-else's-success meltdown to open my eyes.

The fact is we all have different ways we like to plan. While I have no problem planning appointments, luncheons, media appearances, etc. out months in advance, I do have a problem planning my own projects out that far. And that's because I'm

BE OPEN TO HELP FROM OTHERS IN ORDER TO GO FROM IDEA TO DONE

an emotional planner... and I'm a mega action taker. I get jazzed about an idea, grab it out of the ideasphere, have a crazy burst of passion and energy, and create and launch it in a matter of hours. Like when I wrote one of my books in four hours. Or created and published two journals in two days. And how I created 42 checklists in an afternoon and had them ready and selling by the next morning. The energy my passion for the project brought fueled me to create my part in a tight timeframe and pass it off to my team for production. Which brings me to an important point...

Launching any project is easy to do if you have all the writing, graphics, and technical know-how yourself. Not so easy if you rely on a team for much of that setup work, as I do. And you'll quickly learn that to go from idea to done you may very well end up needing the help of others.

The key is to find people who work in your planning style. Are you a plan-it-all-out-six-months-in-advance type of person? Or do you prefer last-minute planning, as I do? The team I have now thrives on last-minute adrenaline, just as I do. The team members love how I work and I love how quickly I can pass a project off to them to put the final technical pieces I need into place. They jump on my projects with enthusiasm the minute I hand them over.

Once you surround yourself with people who work well with your planning style you'll find that success in accomplishing your goals will come quicker and easier.

De-Clutter

It's been scientifically proven that clutter affects the brain's ability to process and actually drains you of energy, keeping your productivity lower than its ultimate potential. Princeton University Neuroscience Institute professors discovered in 2011 that "multiple stimuli present in the visual field at the same time compete for neural representation by mutually suppressing their evoked activity throughout [the] visual cortex, providing a neural correlate for the limited processing capacity of the visual system" (From their report in *The Journal of Neuroscience*, "Interactions of Top-Down and Bottom-Up Mechanisms in Human Visual Cortex").

CLUTTER CREATES CHAOS AND WILL DISTRACT YOU FROM ACCOMPLISHING YOUR GOALS

To simplify what the Princeton professors complicated, what they found is that clutter creates a chaos that results in the constant nagging in the back of your mind to "fix it" instead of spending time working on your project, which will distract you from accomplishing your business goals.

The idea of de-cluttering your life might sound good at first and it can also be incredibly overwhelming. Sure you might love the *idea* of knowing exactly where everything is so that you don't spend an hour hunting for that one pair of sunglasses only to be distracted by everything from that pile of magazines on the floor to the dirty dishes in the sink, but let's be realistic. Organization is a dream. Even people who think they're super organized have one or two areas of their lives that are not. And those who don't think they're organized at all have one or two places where they are... over the top.

For example, I rarely consider myself organized. I have what I call "organized piles" everywhere. And I mean *everywhere*. And then you walk into my art studio and I have every single art supply categorized by media, size, and in some cases, even color. When I started my stained glass studio fresh out of college, my mom walked into my studio and said, "Wow. So now I know where your OCD shows up!" It was then that I realized if I really wanted to, I could be organized.

However try as I might, I still couldn't "get organized" in any other area of my life. It took hiring a professional organizer with a psychology degree to psychoanalyze my organizational style to make me stop beating myself up for being such a slob. She helped me see that my chaotic-looking "organized piles" *were* my style, and that it's totally OK. She started asking me where random things were and I was very specific, as I knew what was in every pile no matter where it landed in my house.

She called it "visual organization" and helped me clean up those piles and organize them into clear bins so I could still see everything, but it was nice, neat, and my floor was clear. I'd finally found a system that worked for me and it's carried over into every room of my home so now (for the most part, unless my husband moves something without telling me... lol) I know where everything is.

If you consider yourself disorganized, all you need to do is find a system that works for you and stick with it. It might be organizing all the books on your shelves by color instead of genre. It might be clear bins and even clear drawers for your clothes instead of a traditional dresser. Or maybe you're like my mom who has to have every spice in her kitchen organized by name so they exactly match the grocery store shelves. Whatever your style, work it. Take the time to set it up and you'll only need to spend a few minutes each day to keep it up.

Train Your Self-Thinking

Did you know you can think yourself *out* of success? What would happen if you started your dream business and suddenly you were getting paid for something you love to do *so much* that it doesn't feel like work? Then things start going wrong... stuff starts breaking, software doesn't work right, and you find yourself struggling to get things done due to all the sudden distractions. Then you start questioning why you decided to start this business to begin with and the next thing you know you're "shoulding" all over yourself saying, "I *should* have handled it this way" or "I *should* have known that would happen."

Every successful entrepreneur knows that the battle for the mind is always raging. It's easy to get caught up in the should... believe me, I know! Just this morning I was shoulding all over myself again until my husband helped me gain some clarity in what was *really* going on. If you find yourself in this downward mental spiral, it's OK. You're human, you're under a lot of pressure as a business owner, and it's totally normal.

THE BATTLE FOR YOUR MIND IS ALWAYS RAGING AND IT'S TOTALLY NORMAL

What's important is for you to see yourself as *who* you want to be, *what* you want to be, and *where* you want to be. Tell yourself every day that you're worthy and valuable. If you have to, write it on your mirror or on sticky notes all over your desk and car. Put it everywhere so you will see it multiple times per day. Training your self-thinking takes time, devotion, and commitment. Once you start down the path of exporting your thoughts you'll find yourself on a lifelong adventure.

The Success Mind-Hack Formula

The first step in the Success Mind-Hack Formula is to become aware. Look around. Be aware of the negative words and phrases you use and how often you repeat them. Be aware of when you start beating yourself down or "shoulding" on yourself. The key to this formula and the most important ingredient is awareness!

Add to your awareness some ass-kicking accountability. Find someone (or a group of someones) to hold you accountable to your goals. To get this book written I created a group program called the Book Writing Challenge. People joined me weekly for an hour live and listened to me type. It sounds weird, but the goals the members and I achieved were nothing short of astounding! I can honestly say that without this group accountability, this book would still be floating around in the ideasphere of my mind just *waiting* for me to pull it down and make it tangible. (Check out BookWritingMonthly.com for what we're up to now!)

The third ingredient to the Success Mind-Hack Formula is coaching. If you don't have a coach, get one. I've had (and still have) a business coach, life coach, money mindset coach, health coach, and karate coach. Without these coaches teaching me what *they* know I wouldn't be anywhere near where I am today. And all these areas play together to help create my success.

Finally, the last ingredient is ACTION. Without action all the mindset changes, accountability, and coaching in the world won't help you. At the end of the day *you* are the *only one responsible for you.* (More on this starting in Chapter 8.)

The number one question you have to ask yourself is, "What is *not* taking action costing me?" My awesome friend, brother-in-love, and former business coach Bob Jenkins said it best, "Take action; revise later!" He's the one who taught me that no product is worth perfection if that means it will never see the light of day and never reach customers' hands. It's better to get your project *done*, reach your goal, launch that new product, and make a few mistakes along the way than not to finish it at all. Mistakes can be fixed. That feeling of failure that you never achieved your biggest dream while on your deathbed can *not* be fixed.

So if nothing else inspires you to take action, think of your death bed. If it's important enough to complete before you die you'll make that goal happen ASAP. If it's not that important and you're OK with the idea of dying with this potentially life-changing dream unfulfilled, then by all means keep up your poor habits, don't make any change in your life, and keep making excuses and blaming everything except your own laziness and lack of motivation.

5

The Upper Realm

The Upper Realm of Asskickonomics is the Realm with which we are the most familiar. It's the "given" realm since the day you were born, when you came into the world completely dependent on someone else. Most accountability comes from this realm where someone "above" you tells you what to do and expects you to follow through with whatever task or assignment you are given. From picking up your toys when you were a toddler to turning in that paper on time to a teacher all the way up to satisfying your duties at your first job and heeding your business coach's advice; the Upper Realm has always been present and will be a part of your existence for as long as you live.

What's tricky about the Upper Realm is that as you grow and mature it actually resides both above *and* below you. You have people in your life who reside in your personal Upper Realm and you may also be in authority over others, which places you in *their* Upper Realms. For example, when teenagers are asked to babysit younger siblings they are inhabiting their siblings' Upper Realms in that they are in charge, and yet their parents are in *their* Upper Realms because they are expected to follow through with the task of keeping their siblings alive and safe until the parents return.

We'll cover the positioning of you in others' Upper Realms later in this book. For now let's explore the relationship you have with your personal Upper Realm; those in authority over you.

Who Goes There?

There are two different types of Upper Realm inhabitants. Those in natural authority over you and those whom you invite to inhabit your Upper Realm for a limited time, whether it be to get their advice in a matter or feedback on a project.

Simply put, those in authority over you may include law enforcement, attorneys, bankers, pastors, elders, counselors, mentors or leaders, coaches, teachers, professors, parents, grandparents, bosses or supervisors, your Sensei at the martial arts school, the local government, and the IRS. Most of these people should be in your personal Upper Realm by default.

When I first began telling my clients about the Upper Realm they immediately identified with one of the most obvious default Upper Realm inhabitants…

Have you ever been driving down the freeway bobbing your head and singing your lungs out to whatever song was on your favorite CD… not paying close attention to your speed… (You know where this story is headed, don't you?), and suddenly you saw flashing blue and red lights in your rear-view mirror? At first you may think it's for someone or something else until the officer in the flashing car directly behind you tweaks his siren. Then your heart begins to race as you realize he wants you to pull over and you're probably going to get a ticket. As you pull over, you may begin to sweat a little and think of where you were headed—perhaps a meeting with a client or on your way to your kid's soccer game—and your mind starts playing the "what excuse can I give" game as you try to come up with a better reason why you'll be late than the truth. Not to mention the ticket the officer starts writing and hands to you through your open window. I've seen the looks on faces of people who have been pulled over and I've experienced it myself (though, thankfully, not in a very long time... but I remember the emotion as if it were yesterday). Some people may even begin to panic if they're driving a borrowed car, or worse, their registration or inspection is out of date.

In this example the person who got pulled over is being hit on multiple sides by inhabitants of the Upper Realm. In that moment the officer represents the law, which you must obey unless you wish to face the consequences. He is also in your personal Upper Realm. The idea of letting down the

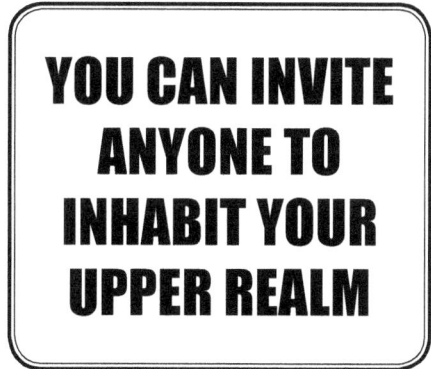

YOU CAN INVITE ANYONE TO INHABIT YOUR UPPER REALM

client due to being late and the resulting guilt places that client temporarily in your Upper Realm as you're giving them Upper Realm power although they naturally do not reside there. In the same way, the feeling of disappointing your kids or spouse puts both the children and the spouse temporarily in the Upper Realm as well. While clients and children usually do not (and should not) reside in your personal Upper Realm of Asskickonomics, they can if you give them permission to do so, as at times you may invite others into your Upper Realm like your spouse or significant other, a friend, or even a client who has expertise you could use to gain feedback on an idea. We'll cover more on this dynamic of Upper Realm abuse in the next chapter. When it comes to your spouse or business partner, in some areas of the relationship you will inhabit each others' Upper Realms. And in a healthy relationship you'll be partners with the same Upper Realms or at least equal Upper Realms.

Ultimately, your personal Upper Realm inhabitants are basically the people who can tell you what to do and when they do you *feel* like you have to do it, whether you actually do have to comply or not. When someone inhabits your Upper Realm and they are invited by you to do so, or they must do so (such as the officer in the story above), they set the guidelines and it's up to you to follow those guidelines. In some cases they also have the authority to kick your ass into submission simply because of the realm they inhabit in relation to you.

THERE WILL ALWAYS BE CONSEQUENCES (GOOD AND BAD) TO YOUR CHOICES

You have the power of choice in every scenario, even with those in your Upper Realm. For example, if you defy the officer in the earlier scenario you may end up in a holding cell. You still have the choice to defy him and he has the choice and power to lock you up should you make that choice. In these cases, if you don't abide by the rules of those in your Upper Realm you may experience discomfort, anxiety, or worse, and regret your disobedience.

The Upper Realm typically shows up for the entrepreneur when you hire a business coach, a marketing expert, or have a run-in with the IRS. You still have choices and there are consequences (both good and bad) to those choices.

The Upper Realm's Purpose

If you let them, your Upper Realm inhabitants can cause much fear and anxiety or they can bring you freedom. Freedom you desperately long for to finally be yourself. Freedom to *choose* to accept the consequences of disobedience or to abide by their guidelines. Freedom to take your personal power back and fully to live into your success and own your accomplishments. Freedom to take responsibility for both your failures and your awesomeness. Because those in your Upper Realm know that to fulfill your purpose and bring your mission to those you serve through your business, you must fully own who you are and what you've accomplished thus far. And only when you discover that mindset switch and turn it on will you tap into your full potential.

Those in your Upper Realm are there to help you fulfill one of the most important purposes in your life—to challenge you to show up to every expected and unexpected situation you face in life and business with your full potential. Many times your Upper Realm inhabitants can see your potential when you are completely oblivious to it. And if they're doing their job right they will point it out to you—with or without your permission. Because an appointed or invited Upper Realm inhabitant who *deserves* to be there knows that you will *only* kick ass in your life and business by showing up to your potential.

The Upper Realm's Danger Zone

Most people don't use their Upper Realm to grow and feed their success because it's much easier to run from a challenge given by the Upper Realm than to embrace it. No human enjoys being vulnerable or uncomfortable. Yet if the challenge holds any value for you to grow as a person and expand your business, it will not be comfortable... as you probably already know. In fact the easiest thing to do when faced with an Upper Realm challenge is to convince yourself that you tried your best (even if you didn't really try at all) and say to yourself, "Well, that didn't work." Then you promptly place someone else in that Upper Realm position, effectively dethroning the previous inhabitant whose challenge was too uncomfortable for you to face head-on. If you've seen strug-gling entrepreneurs jump from program to program and coach to coach, never really seeming to make any progress with their business, this is a sure sign that they are ignoring those in their Upper Realm. It's much more difficult, yet a *lot* more rewarding, to actually consider the challenge and meet it.

I remember in my early consulting days I sat down with a woman I met through a networking group and offered to help her with her business... for free (Mistake #1). I outlined a plan for her, including re-branding her amazing skincare products because nobody could read the labels, much less know what they were. This woman worked a day job and jumped from MLM company to the next hot network marketing gadget in hopes of "striking it big someday." Yet she had this incredible potential locked inside herself with her unique skin care formulas and a corner on the market I'd never seen anyone tap into before. I told her she could quit her job and do it full time if she got her shit together. She thanked me and we stayed in touch, yet other than changing her labels to be more readable she didn't follow any of my other advice... for three whole years.

We temporarily lost touch and I figured since I hadn't seen her at any of the local events (and I started speaking and traveling more myself) that she was still at that same job. Three years later I saw her at a trade show. She had a beautiful table and was following *every guideline* I had laid out for her so many years prior. I chatted with her and told her how proud I was to see her success. That's when she told me that she didn't know what happened or why she couldn't get it before, but within the past month everything had come together in her mind and she could finally *see* what I was talking about three years earlier. She told me that she wasn't ready to give up her job security blanket at that time and she just couldn't see how what she had was worth anything, so she kept doing the same thing for almost three whole years expecting a different result and not really getting anywhere. Then something clicked inside for her and she eliminated the rest of her MLM businesses to focus on her skin care line, found the notes she took from our meeting back then, and put them into practice.

Within one month she was full time with her business. And she told me that her one regret was that it took so long for her to "see" in herself what I saw in her from that first meeting. I saw her potential and believed in her. But she had to believe in herself to take the homework I gave her and put it into practice. And *that* is the power of the Upper Realm—if the people in it are properly placed and their advice is followed.

The Upper Realm Power

As an entrepreneur, one inhabitant that may consistently be invited to your personal Upper Realm is a business coach. I'm a firm believer that *every* entrepreneur (and wantrepreneur!) *needs* a coach. I've had several business coaches throughout my entrepreneurial life. Each one has served a specific purpose to help me with a distinct problem. Most of my coaches have challenged me to think differently, try new tools, test new strategies, etc. Not all of them were comfortable. Many of them I resisted… some for years. In fact I knew these challenges were designed to stretch me and as a result of that stretching I would be more successful and more effective, yet I still went kicking and screaming into many of them… sometimes for years before I leapt. If you've ever taken a Yoga class you know that stretching is not always comfortable. It's not

STRETCHING IS DESIGNED TO CHALLENGE YOU AND HELP YOU GROW

designed to be! It's designed to challenge you, to pull your body in new directions, and to help you do things you've never done before. The same can be said of emotional and spiritual growth. The pain of stretching is what we call "up-leveling" in the business world and it's almost never easy. And actually I would go so far as to say if it were easy it would not be stretching you in a way that would actually help you achieve your goals. And yet when done properly (almost always with a little pain or at least tears of clarity), it's rewarding beyond belief!

When I first started working with my personal trainer I thought I was physically broken. My legs have been bent my entire life and my knees faced each other. This deformity was the source of ridicule from bullies throughout my school days and phys-ical education classes were a nightmare. I even had times when the teacher pointed out how "stupid" I was when I ran... due to my deformed legs. In addition to them being bent, they were a constant source of pain. I remember when I was about seven years old I collapsed while walking across my back yard. I was in agonizing pain and I could no longer feel my left leg, knee, or toes. My parents argued over what to do and finally decided to take me to see a chiropractor. Now whatever your personal opinions are about chiropractic, I'm grateful for it (and I still go to one today). My father carried me into the office and I walked out on my own. From then on I managed the pain... as it was still constantly there.

Many years later I met Glenn, the trainer who said he could "fix" me. For two years I didn't believe him; then I finally broke down and worked with him. Within two *days* of working on the physical therapy-style exercises he had me do, my left knee became almost completely straight. Within a few weeks my left leg straightened out. After three months my right knee was almost straight. My legs were no longer bowed in! Now if I hadn't seen such results I would have given up within the first week. Because the pain was intense. I was forcing my body to react and stretch in directions it never had before. I was retraining my muscles to define what was healthy and straight, healing old injuries, and literally bending the structure of my lower body into a healthier position. If you've ever broken a bone and had to go through physical therapy, you know the pain can be excruciating.

And yet, the power of someone in the Upper Realm kicking my ass into submission to stick with the program yielded the most amazing results I've seen in my life. The pain dramatically reduced and my legs are no longer an embarrassment. And the best part? For the first time in my martial arts life I can do a proper side kick. Not only *do* one, but perform it perfectly... *without* pain... something I'd *never* been able to do before! The very first side-kick I performed, I literally fell to the mats in my home Dojo and started to cry. I saw it as a miracle. And I instantly recognized that without the power of the Upper Realm I never would have lived to see that day.

6

Upper Realm Abuse

In the last chapter, I touched on a concept I call Upper Realm abuse. This is the scenario that often happens right before you start to feel resentment toward someone. It often starts with you saying "yes" to someone that places them temporarily in your Upper Realm, even when that little voice inside warns you not to. Call it instinct, intuition, and the like; it's the voice we often ignore in favor of what we hope will be a better outcome than the warning suggests. And ignoring that little voice almost *always* ends in the way we fear… the way we know deep down inside that it will end.

An Upper Realm Abuse Story

I don't often tell this story as it's still a little raw. When my parents first split up, my dad turned toward me for "support" (I use that term *very* loosely). What he wanted was a free place to stay, someone to cook his meals and take care of him, and someone to listen to him tell all his life's woes. It got to the point that he was calling me several times per hour and if I didn't pick up the phone, he'd keep calling until I did rather than leave me a message. Whether I was driving, in a meeting, or with a client, the phone would ring or vibrate until I either answered it or turned it off. At one point I was fumbling for it in the car while driving because it was the fifth time he'd called in as many minutes, so I was concerned it was an emergency. As I grabbed the ringing phone, I swerved away from a parked car and answered, concerned and scared that I'd almost rammed someone else's car.

> # A COMMON MISCONCEPTION ABOUT THE UPPER REALM IS THAT YOUR PARENTS ALWAYS INHABIT IT

He told me that all he wanted to do was let me know about a job interview that went well. To say I was furious is an understatement. Due to his persistent calling and my concern that he was injured or worse (his mind wasn't in the right place at the time), I nearly hit a parked car and got injured myself. He didn't want to listen to how I was upset at the relentless phone calls and how while I wanted to celebrate with him, I also wanted to live my own life. Instead he said, "Well, I thought you'd be happy for me" and other common guilt-manipulation speak. It got to the point that I couldn't handle my time and space being monopolized and I recognized that the emotional abuse my mom put up with for so many years was now being turned on me.

So in one of our final conversations together I drew a line in the sand. I refused to be that caretaker, even for my father, who by default had inhabited my Upper Realm much of my life. I saw that choice as enabling the same behavior that pushed my mom away, to which he ultimately admitted. I felt the resentment grow inside me each time I saw his name pop up on my phone screen and I knew something was wrong. When I finally confronted him and set a boundary with how he was treating me and monopolizing my time, his only response was, "Where did you learn to set such good boundaries? I respect that." What's ironic is that he's the one that taught me how to respect myself and demand how I wanted to be treated.

A common misconception about the Upper Realm is that your parents *always* inhabit it. While your parents do inhabit this realm by default when you're born, once you become an adult you get to choose if or when they take up that position in your life again. It's part of the process of growing up. And unfortunately, many family members will always see you as "Little Insert-Your-Name-Here," not the grown adult capable of making your own powerful decisions. As soon as you re-open your Upper Realm to them to inhabit, they will contribute to a co-dependency Normalcy Trap and you'll never feel like you're "good enough" to make it on your own. This creates an unhealthy scenario for both of you, which is why learning to own your awesomeness and powerful place in the world is so important.

Family, friends, your spouse or significant other, children (yours and others'), clients, employees, and even co-workers can all take up a position of authority in your Upper Realm *if you let them*. However, they don't deserve a zip code there. Sometimes you may go to them for advice, accountability, or encouragement, and at that time you're inviting them to *temporarily* take a place in your Upper Realm. In those moments it's important for you to remember that they inhabit that realm at *your* invitation, not by right or entitlement. Once you give people a position in your Upper Realm it's easy for them to assert themselves there long term, even if that positioning becomes unhealthy for you. It's a taste of power and they will tend to remain there as long as the reason you invited them there still exists... and sometimes even when it doesn't.

The Boundary Equation

I read a book in college related to Upper Realm abuse that I credit as being *the* book that propelled me on the path of personal growth and development. It was so powerful and life-changing for me that I've not only recommended it to hundreds of my students, but I've also bought dozens of copies and given them away. *Boundaries*, by Henry Cloud and John Townsend, has been a continuous go-to source for me since the first day I discovered it when I was a Sophomore in college. While it's written from a Christian perspective and therefore it may not appeal to everyone, the principles in it are sound advice for all who struggle with feelings of resentment and anyone who has an issue saying "no" to friends, family, and anyone else improperly inhabiting their Upper Realm. In this book, Cloud and Townsend take the reader on a practical journey through common boundary problems, how boundaries are typically developed as children (and often not developed at all), and how to establish those boundaries in your own life even if you've allowed people access to your Upper Realm for long periods of time and they've not only set up shop, but have years' worth of "advice" stacked up to use as ammunition against any argument you have for removing them from their lofty position.

BOUNDARIES ARE ESSENTIAL TO DEVELOP DEEP RELATIONSHIPS WITH OTHERS

Boundaries are essential to developing deep and meaningful relationships with others. They help us to feel safe and to give others a clear "yes" and "no" for how we expect to be treated. I recently had to set a boundary with a friend. We would often banter back and forth and I had made a promise to him that I hadn't had the chance to deliver on yet. He took that as a cue to badger me some more, only this time I felt he took it too far. When I read his email full of bullshit insults and accusations (his description of what he sent), I was pissed. Not upset, *pissed*. I took it *very* personally, which was the first sign something was amiss. I had never let him know where my boundaries were and how far his "joking" could go, so I couldn't really blame him for pushing against that fence, but that didn't stop me from trying. My reaction to that single email was the source of a very heated discussion with my husband who knew what our friend meant by it and had trouble wrapping his head around what would make me so upset.

What hurt wasn't the experience itself, but the result, which made me realize a few uncomfortable things about myself. First, I have to be clear in letting others know how I expect to be treated, even when it's done in jest or in the name of fun. Second, my father was the same way in that he would use banter and humor to belittle others. They took it as an attack; he saw it as funny. I recognized the triggers that were pulled inside me regarding how my dad treated others in comparison to how I was being treated at that moment and I used that moment to heal the portion of my fence that I'd allowed my father to rip down so many years before My friend stepped right through that same fence because it had a gaping hole in it.

And finally, I stopped making assumptions that others would know where my boundaries were and flat-out told this friend how I felt. He responded in kindness with an apology and confirmed what I already knew, that he didn't "mean" any harm and he understood that there was a fence he had pushed through. If I had not communicated where my boundaries were with him, to this day I'd remain pissed and feel anxiety any time I saw his name pop up on my phone or in my email. I cared too much about the relationship to allow my taking his actions personally to damage our friendship further. And while I had invited him to inhabit my

Upper Realm for a time, it was an invitation to visit, not stay. So I had to make that clear in order to keep our friendship intact.

When you feel your buttons being pushed and start holding resentment toward someone else, it's an emotional sign that something is not right; that usually a boundary has been violated. Either you have an invisible boundary that nobody (even you) knows about until it's breached or it's a boundary others do know about and against which they intentionally push. If this friend had continued to push through that fence when I told him where it was clearly marked it would have turned from boundary testing to bullying. And bullying is where Upper Realm abuse thrives.

Handling Upper Realm Bullies

My husband and I often encounter emotional bullies in our training businesses. It's a lot easier to stay hidden behind a computer screen and push against someone's fences than it is to confront them in person. So unfortunately Upper Realm abuse runs rampant in our online business worlds. From customers who don't receive an answer from our customer support center within a few minutes of submitting it—on a weekend or holiday—to the wannabes who continually see what we're creating and attempt to underhand us with a competitive product, these people are easy to find on the internet. Usually the impatient customers can be handled through gentle communication. But sometimes they get a taste of the "power" they think they hold over us due to having paid for a product or service so they push those boundaries just like a two-year-old until we say, "No." And often the anger and resentment starts to show on our part before we realize we've let it go too far and suddenly we realize that we've allowed them a solid landing pad in our Upper Realms.

Clients and customers pay you for a specific product or service and many times they may *expect* much more of your personal time than is included. And if you don't give it to them due to a boundary you may feel guilty because money is involved. I had one customer purchase a training course from me and she kept posting requests for my personal advice on her business in the Facebook group. While I encourage questions, comments, and celebratory links to products they create in my group, I'm very clear that I don't offer one-on-one coaching within the group setting. The group is for mutual accountability between all my students with me there as a monitor, not as a hand-holding coach. This particular woman expected me to deliver one-on-one coaching to her instead of going through the course she purchased and seeking her answers there.

At first I felt guilty about not honoring her wishes, but I set my boundary with her anyway as I noticed I was slowly allowing her ground in my Upper Realm and she was seeing that as an invitation to own a piece of it. This was someone I did not wish to invite into my Upper Realm at all—a client who expected

SET SOLID BOUNDARIES EVEN IF YOU FEEL GUILTY FOR DOING IT

more from me than she had paid for—so I re-stated my policy. She publicly accosted and any guilt I had initially felt quickly faded as her bully colors showed.

Some of my colleagues may have said I was being mean or that she was a paying customer and the "customer is always right," but I beg to differ. If I had "helped" her and wasted my time and energy feeling resentment for allowing her across the boundary into my Upper Realm where she felt she could dictate how I spent my time late on a Sunday night, I would not have been honoring my integrity to myself and the policies I've put in place to protect my time and energy. This means I would have ended up with *less* time and energy, not to mention motivation, to help my other paying customers who legitimately paid for my one-on-one time.

Upholding my Upper Realm boundary and not allowing her to monopolize my time (which is a form of abuse) may have temporarily made her upset, but just like that two-year-old throwing her temper tantrum, eventually she learned to respect the boundary or move on to learn from someone else who doesn't have those same fences in place. And both ways I win as I'm not attached to whether she continues to be my customer or not, but I am attached to wanting what's best for my personal mental health and my desire to serve all my customers in the best way that I can.

NO ONE SHOULD INHABIT YOUR UPPER REALM WITHOUT YOUR PERMISSION

While I believe in the mantra "under promise and over deliver," it is possible for you as an entrepreneur to "over deliver" yourself straight into debt, bankruptcy, anxiety, depression, or worse. If you are bombarded by going "above and beyond" for your clients and customers to the point of resentment then something is wrong. You may think you're helping them, but all you're doing is enabling them to bully you over and over again by tearing down sections of your fences and allowing them through.

This also goes for everyone else who should not inhabit your Upper Realm without your explicit permission. And even in the case of your spouse or significant other, if you invite them to inhabit your Upper Realm for any purpose or length of time make sure your boundaries with how they can use that space are extremely clear. If you are unclear with how you want to be treated you can't blame your spouse for walking across and invisible fence.

Communicate. Explain how you want to be treated and what you desire for your relationship.

The Upper Realm can be a tricky place to navigate. While some people reside there by default and there may be severe negative consequences to not following their rules, others reside there purely by your invitation. Those you invite must have clear fences to indicate how far they can travel within the Realm. Think of a farm with a fence that keeps the dogs away from the chickens. You are responsible for that fence, not the dogs. So if the dogs cross a boundary you think is there but you did not make clear, they may wreak havoc on the chickens.

It's the same in your Upper Realm. You may invite a dog into your space and at first he's cute, fluffy, cuddly, and enjoyable to have there. You respect his contribution to your life *until* he crosses a line and gets into the garbage, or worse, eats one of your chickens. Suddenly you're mad at the dog and threaten to take him to the pound. OK that may be a bit extreme, but you get my point. Whose fault was it that the dog ransacked the garbage or attacked a chicken? Was it the dog's, with his built-in instincts to hunt for food or protect his humans from that big scary metal can? No. It's your fault for not putting a fence in place to make it clear to your dog where he's to play and what areas are off limits.

This same guideline applies to your clients. You may have clients with expertise you can use to benefit your company. For example, I'm a client for my housekeepers and I'm also a consultant for their company. In this way they have invited me to inhabit their Upper Realm so that I may give them advice and they can choose to follow it or not. With their permission I may increase my stake in their Upper Realm by becoming an investor in their company and helping them grow it beyond what they can do alone. When money changes hands like that, boundaries and expectations *must* be set for all involved so I know where my fences lie in their Upper Realm and don't cross those lines. The Upper Realm is the only realm that needs boundaries for those who are invited, as they will come and go at will, pitch a tent, build a house, or possibly own a zip code there without clear boundaries on where their position ends and someone else's begins.

When you begin to set these boundaries and help those you've invited in your Upper Realm to navigate them, at first you may feel guilty and that's totally normal. The guilt will fade the more you hold true to your boundaries and recognize the power making those decisions gives you to create better relationships with everyone, no matter what realm they inhabit.

7

Obscure Upper Realm Inhabitants

Sometimes you may get a motivational push in a new direction (whether you want to go that way or not) from obscure Upper Realm inhabitants. These are the peers, co-workers, possible business partners, acquaintances, and others who come across your path when you least expect them to and who hold Upper Realm authority in relation to you, even if they make less money than you or are working on a different set of goals and have different aspirations. These are the people you may look to for inspiration, support, and camaraderie, and who have the power to say, "No" or to recommend another course of action for you to take.

My good friend Melissa's random experience with a neighbor is an example of how an obscure Upper Realm inhabitant assumed the authority to motivate her to live out her calling. She posted this story on Facebook and I was thrilled when she said I could share it in this book.

"I saw this lady power walk every day. I mean, she spent hours and hours doing this... *every day!* I watched her come home from work and she'd always be amazingly dressed. One day as I was on my balcony and saw her walking around the corner I yelled, 'YOU LOOK AMAZING!'

"'Who said that?' she yelled back. I knew she couldn't see me and as she came running back around the corner she said, 'Thank you, I've just let myself go! I'm a single mother of three kids and it's hard. I *have* to lose 50 pounds and I'm down 25 already.'

"I grabbed my phone and showed her my personal side-by-side photos of what 50 pounds lost looked like. She started crying and said, 'Thank you for the motivation. I really need motivation. I'm doing this by myself and I just keep thinking *5K a day, just 5K a day.*' I couldn't help myself, so I grabbed all the motivational resources I've gathered for my own weight loss journey and gave them to her. As I left she said, 'If you ever see me again, feel free to yell, cheer, and motivate me.'

"Tomorrow morning I plan to purposely be outside to either join her or cheer her on or even play something motivational, because we all need a support system. NONE OF US should be out there trying to reach goals ourselves. NO ONE!!! The quickest, easiest, most effective way to results is commitment... and even that's only 20%. The other 80% is support!"

Melissa's neighbor challenged her to stay motivated and to continue to motivate others. The exchange they had enabled her to be an inspiration to her neighbor and her neighbor in turn to be an inspiration to Melissa's life goal of motivating others. This woman was an obscure Upper Realm inhabitant in that she unexpectedly came into Melissa's life and motivated her to continue to be the inspiration she's called to be.

> **UPPER REALM INHABITANTS OFTEN SHOW UP AS PEERS**

In many cases Upper Realm inhabitants show up as peers—equals—yet they still hold some power to help you say, "Yes" to an action you need to take to achieve success. They may be on the same journey as you, on a journey you recently completed, or even on a journey you know is coming soon for yourself. In any case they still hold some sort of authority over you, whether that's a motivational authority, inspirational authority, or even an obscure fellow business authority.

Let me explain that last one... Sometimes the Upper Realm's obscure inhabitants are people you'd think would be your peers, but actually have authority in some area over you. And if they say, "No," you may have to find another option or just roll with it. This happened to me when my husband and I opened our toy store *Toy Box Gifts & Wonder* in downtown Chambersburg, PA.

There was one toy line that I *really* wanted to carry in our store. One that I'd wanted to have for the past few years, since I first became aware of it. And the candy shop across the street carried that line. So in the ever-present interest of working together (I believe in coopetition, not competition) I approached the owner of the candy shop to see how we might work together and *both* carry this line of toys for the mutual benefit of both of us cross-promoting each other.

In my brief meeting with him he admitted that his gift section was merely an impulse buy section for people who came in strictly to buy candy, so I immediately felt good about my proposal. I proposed to him that I carry a small part of the line in our store that he did not yet carry, and we could refer business back and forth. While timidly resistant at first, he started to get excited at the idea of partnering, as I would refer people to his shop to pick up the more popular items, thus referring business his way. I saw this agreement as a clear boundary and I temporarily invited him to inhabit my Upper Realm, as since he already had the account with this vendor, the final decision was his. We shook hands, he said he would call his rep (the same rep I had) and that he would let me know what his next order would be, which he was placing in the next couple of days. I went on my merry way excited about the possibilities of this partnership.

The next day I got a very short email from him stating that he had thought about it overnight and would not partner with us on this line of toys. This reaction was completely unexpected and in that moment he became an obscure inhabitant of my Upper Realm, since I had invited him there with the proposal of partnership. Suddenly there was nothing I could do to carry that line as the answer was, "NO." The decision was made, it was final, and I'd invited it by creating space in my Upper Realm for him to temporarily inhabit. And while at first I was angry at the result, I did understand *why* he made that decision. In this case while he was my peer in business and in no way in direct authority of what I could do, say, or how I could conduct business, he *was* an obscure inhabitant of my Upper Realm in what I could do with this one particular line of toys.

> ## ALLOW OBSCURE UPPER REALM INHABITANTS TO MOTIVATE YOU BY CHALLENGING YOUR NORMALCY TRAPS

Obscure Upper Realm inhabitants can be beneficial to your success, as they unexpectedly motivate you to take action toward your dream. They can challenge your Normalcy Trap and they can also close doors and encourage you to discover another path. I decided to hunt for another similar line of toys that was exclusive only to my shop, that no one else in town would be able to carry. As a result of the door that he shut, I found several lines of "impulse buy" toys that have been extremely successful for us. I would not have thought to look for some of them if that door had remained open. And yes, I promptly kicked him out of his temporary Upper Realm residence.

Whether an obscure Upper Realm inhabitant is instrumental for opening doors for you or closing them, understand that you always have the ability to forge your own path. Some doors may shut and remain shut. Some things you want to do may not come to pass due to these obscure Upper Realm inhabitants calling the shots. And some ways you discover around those closed doors may open you up to another avenue of success you've only ever dreamed about!

8

The Inner Realm

Confession time... I don't want to write today. As I sit down to write this chapter I can list about a dozen things I'd rather be doing. Things like checking the mail, sitting in my chair in the sunroom sipping tea, reading a book unrelated to research for this book, walking through the addition being built onto our house, unboxing toys for our store downtown, taking a nap, playing with the cats... The list goes on and on and on.

Frankly I don't want to force my butt to stay in this chair until my scheduled hour of writing time is up. But I know if I break my habit of holding a "writing date" with myself each week it'll be easier to keep that habit broken the next time. And skip it the time after that. And before I know it this book will still be partially written on my hard drive a year after my goal of having it completed has passed.

That's not going to work for me... and I'm sure since you're reading this it wouldn't have worked for you, either! So this is my ultimate "get-my-ass-in-the-chair-and-just-write-it-already" moment. I have a decision to make. I can force myself to sit here and write and get in the groove I've apparently found venting about my own frustrations about writing, and use it as the perfect example of how to access the Inner Realm of Asskickonomics... or I can just say to hell with it and run like the wind in the other direction.

The Choice

You're reading this now, so obviously I chose to find my zone and write. Why? Because first I have a goal to get this book done. And second, if you don't learn how to activate your Inner Realm of Asskickonomics, you'll remain stuck in your Normalcy Trap of complacency with your dreams and goals always being "someday" visions instead of "today" actions. Of all the realms of Asskickonomics, the Inner Realm is the hardest to negotiate. It's much easier to say, "Oh yeah, you're right" to someone in authority in the Upper Realm and to take instant action while they hold you accountable than it is to make yourself set your ass in your chair and do it. It's even relatively easy to listen to the point of view of someone in the Lower Realm (more on that in Chapter 15). But to listen to your *self?* Well, that's the hardest thing of all. Speaking of one of the most common goals—fitness — KISS guitarist Paul Stanley said it best, "Quite honestly, I don't think most people are motivated enough to do what they need to on their own. You either need a spotter or you need a trainer. You need somebody there to push you to get that extra five."

Call it self-motivation, self-worth, personal drive, what-have-you... the fact is Paul was right. Motivating your *self* to take action is incredibly difficult. I've said it before: human beings are not meant to do anything in life alone. We're creatures of community. We survive together and thrive together. So accountability coming from any external source feels more natural and is an easier yes. And yet there's this one realm of Asskickonomics that while it's the most difficult to put into practice, is actually the most powerful... the Inner Realm. This is the realm where you have to call the shots on yourself. You have to pep talk yourself, convince yourself, motivate yourself, and kick your own ass. You have to do what it takes to get what you want... *yourself.* You have to *drive* yourself toward that finish line, because at the end of the day you're the only one left to make your*self* take action.

When nobody else is around, if *you* don't take the action necessary to kick your own ass, you'll find yourself popping bonbons in front of the TV and burying yourself in binging the next eleven episodes of your favorite sitcom, while your dreams remain ideas posted on sticky notes around your computer in the other room.

The Power of the Inner Realm

Without the Inner Realm of Asskickonomics, entrepreneurs wouldn't accomplish any of their goals. Why? Because while we're designed for community and having our asses kicked by someone else is a great motivator, the fact is the only person you can count on to *always* be there no matter what is yourself. After you hang up the phone with your coach, you are stuck with *you.* After you leave a staff meeting, you're alone with *you.* You can't escape *you* when you go home after your day job and start working on your passion business. You can sequester yourself in a beachside cottage to get away from the world or lock yourself in the bathroom for five minutes of peace and quiet at home, but you're still in there with your *self.* And as soon as you recognize the amazingness that is always being with someone else—YOU—and give your *self* the power to self-motivate, you'll make progress on your dreams beyond what you can possibly imagine.

> **THE ONLY PERSON YOU CAN NEVER ESCAPE BEING WITH IS YOU**

That. Is. Powerful.

Because at the end of the day, if you learn how to motivate your*self* effectively, you will be **unstoppable**. And to be a success in business you *must* be unstoppable. You must be a force to be reckoned with. Because gale-force winds of change and uncer-

LEARN HOW TO MOTIVATE YOURSELF AND YOU WILL BE UNSTOPPABLE

tainty *will* blow all around you and if you stay rooted to what you know to be true for yourself and tie those roots to the powerful self-accountability of the Inner Realm, you won't waver. The earth may shift, but you'll remain steadfast and strong and pursue your goals no matter what. And *that* will make you unstoppable.

My Personal Windstorm

My initial goal was to finish writing the messy rough draft for this book six months after I started actively writing it. It's why I created the Book Writing Challenge and brought others on board to work on their projects alongside me. And yet while the community was there with all of us working together at the same time on our respective projects, and while we each made significant progress, I'm sitting here just *starting* to write the third major portion of this book in the final 45 minutes of the challenge. I did not complete my initial goal as I still have six chapters left to write and two more started that I need to finish. Why didn't I meet my goal? Isn't six months more than enough time to write a book?

I'd like to say it's because I've lived through my own personal windstorms these past six months. Gale after gale blew across, pushing me in other directions and leaving this manuscript perpetually open in a neglected file on my laptop. My personal Normalcy Trap is procrastination. While I work well under tight deadlines, I also have a habit of biting off more than I can chew with any given project... and sometimes the goal is a lot bigger than the time I've allotted to complete it. Can you relate? It's not like you're sitting around twiddling your thumbs. Like I have been, you probably get easily distracted by a multitude of other projects... and your passion goal just hasn't become important enough to you yet to finish, so it sits there stoically on your computer screen or desk just waiting for you to take notice of it again.

While I've been writing this particular book, my husband and I have opened our first brick and mortar business, *Toy Box Gifts & Wonder*, a STEAM-focused toy store in our local downtown of Chambersburg, PA. I hired two full-time employees, two part-timers, and two seasonal temps, all of whom needed training. We signed the lease and began construction on our *second* brick and mortar store, *Nerdvana Outpost*, a nerdy gift shop on the opposite end of Main St. from our first store... and I'm in charge of finding and ordering the inventory for both stores... which is a seemingly never-ending full-time job all on its own (though it's a ton of fun too). I also launched my first e-comm site, Fluffy Cat Stuff, with three products I designed myself, created and taught seven brand new multi-module courses and 28 weekly Mastermind training sessions under my brand *The Book Ninja*, spoke at a couple of events, became a Certified Play Expert with the American Specialty Toy Retailing Association, attended two conferences, joined the Advisory Council for PENN State Mont Alto LaunchBox, our new entrepreneur incubator in town, joined the Downtown Design Committee for downtown revitalization, taught a month-long challenge for this book (grab your spot free at AssKickingChallenge.com), helped set up and work two downtown festivals for our store (as well as about 10 other store events), and this weekend I'm traveling across the country for a week to attend a high-level mastermind event… on which I hope to finish this manuscript. Because what else would I do on two five-hour flights?

All that has happened in just the past six months, not counting anything more I'm going to do before this book is finished and published, including fourth-quarter events and management for our toy store. Whew! Writing it all down and reading it makes me feel a bit overwhelmed and tired, and if it does the same for you, sit up straight and take a deep breath. Because here's the thing. Most of the time I feel like I've been slacking… in part because I've made time to binge watch a few of my favorite shows like *Outlander*, *The Profit*, *Shark Tank*, and *Stranger Things*, and while I often see TV watching as a necessary evil for me to unplug from "real life" for a bit, but I still consider it a waste of time. I've learned the power of delegation, living in my own genius to focus on my strengths, and unless I have a pressing deadline or an active project I feel like I'm a total slacker.

For me personally, my Inner Realm is so strong it continually pushes me to do more, be more, see more, and learn more. In those few moments when I do watch TV I often have my iPad with me to jot down random business ideas as they come. The other night I outlined an entire new three-month consulting program while watching the *Big Bang Theory*. My work IS my life (more on this in Chapter 14). And I feel like if I were to live any other way I'd be bored out of my mind. It takes a certain level of strength to keep up this pace and to continually push myself beyond the boundaries of my personal Normalcy Trap. And if you're a seasoned entrepreneur or even just starting out, you probably understand what I'm talking about.

Your friends and family may never understand what drives you. Hell, *you* may never understand what drives you. Just know that what you see in the lives of successful entrepreneurs is this strength: the deep roots of accountability and the tall confidence of achieving their goals. What most people don't see are the strong windstorms that tried with every ounce of energy they had to knock that success down, rip apart that confidence, and shatter those roots. These winds may show

SUCCESSFUL ENTREPRENEURS GROW DEEP ROOTS OF ACCOUNTABILITY

up as unexpected "life" circumstances, such as illness or relationship divisions. Or they may just be the common distractions of everyday living, or even as in my case, new businesses being started and current ones growing. Whatever their source, the magic ingredient in the secret sauce to every successful entrepreneur's achievement of their dreams is to dig deep and establish those roots in a way that allows them to outlast, outshine, and outmaneuver anything life throws at them. Without the roots of the Inner Realm holding your tree of dreams steady it will blow over, fall, crumble, and rot.

Then you'll be left shaking your head, wondering what happened, and why you just can't "get ahead" in business. Stay tuned as we take the next few chapters to deep-dive into the Inner Realm of Asskickonomics.

9

What It **Really** *Takes*

The Inner Realm of Asskickonomics is the magic ingredient in the secret sauce to success. While the world sees the outward "overnight" success of an entrepreneur, it doesn't see the self-motivating ass-kicking it took for that success to happen "overnight." People easily see the publicity, money, power, and the popularity. What's almost impossible to see is the *years* of work, the late-night hours, the immediate action-taking on a 3:00 a.m. idea, the "I don't feel like it, but I'm going to do it anyway" drive entrepreneurs *must* have to succeed. They don't see the seven days per week entrepreneurs worked for three or four years straight which allowed them to "suddenly" enjoy two weeks off or a flexible travel schedule once they became "overnight" successes.

We recently had a conversation with one of our employees who wanted an extra day off for a minor holiday in addition to the two days per month we allow our employees to miss work for any reason. My husband responded with, "Isn't every day a work day?" which to the entrepreneur is so totally true! The employee responded with, "When you work Thanksgiving, Christmas, or New Years I'll believe you." Here's the thing... this employee doesn't see us "after hours" or on holidays. He doesn't see the drive, the motivation, the brainstorming, the impulse-working, the idea generating, and the late-night deadline-meeting that happens in "off" time. He doesn't see that while we rarely watch TV, we typically choose business shows like *Billion Dollar Buyer*, *Shark Tank*, *The Profit*, or *The Partner* (with the occasional favorite show as it becomes available and we need a mental break). He never sees how as we watch the drama unfold on the screen we're also analyzing, discussing, plotting, and planning for our own businesses and gauging the reactions of show participants and reasons why they fight an idea or concept presented by the show host(s). He doesn't see the walks through Target when we discuss product packaging design, marketing placement, the new products that don't seem to be selling vs. the ones that jump off the shelves as we analyze why. He doesn't see the 3:00 a.m. idea wake-up calls that get us out of bed and onto our computers to create a new product or implementing a new idea. (Why does that always seem to happen right around 3:00 a.m.?)

The fact is most of the world is terribly naive in what it views as success. People see the outward appearance of fancy cars, a nice house, and free time to travel and want it. And they want it without doing the work; without paying their dues the way the successful have done. They feel entitled and say things like, "That must be nice" to those hard-working entrepreneurs who worked seven days a week for three years and were excited about spending a week away with a loved one. Their conversations with others of similar mindset often include questions like, "I mean if the 'rich' have so much money they should give it to

> **MOST OF THE WORLD IS TERRIBLY NAIVE IN WHAT IT VIEWS AS SUCCESS**

us too, right?" They don't see the amount of work that goes into creating those riches, so somehow they have it in their heads that the rich don't deserve to be rich. They don't understand that for a company to function it needs a cash reserve equal to one year of expenses, because in the business world *nothing* is guaranteed. What works today might not work tomorrow. Every day is an unknown variable and if they see a number they can't comprehend in the business bank account, their first thought is, "And they can't give me more hours or a raise?!" They also don't realize that businesses and entrepreneurs are the very backbone of a thriving economy and that without them providing jobs the economy would collapse. Basically, employees of these companies often take their jobs for granted, expect more for less, and never, ever realize just how much time, energy, and effort the entrepreneur puts into making their business a success.

For the non-successful or those wired only to be worker bees for someone else, it's a lot easier to say, "screw it, I'm tired" and veg out in front of the TV all evening than it is to stay up late at night and put the finishing touches on a new product. It's easier to laugh with the latest sitcom or watch a reality show where people eat worms than it is to pick up the business book when their eyes are already tired after a

> **IT'S EASIER TO SAY "SCREW IT, I'M TIRED" THAN IT IS TO DO WHAT IT TAKES TO FINISH A PROJECT**

long day at their "job." It's easier to stick with the 9–5 and keep their weekends as play dates with their friends to go out drinking than it is to work until midnight or 2:00 a.m. every weekday just to keep pushing those same hours through the weekend. And that, my friend, is why most "entrepreneurs" are actually *want*repreneurs who never see the amount of success they're capable of. They don't do what it takes, they get tired, and they expect others to hand them what they really want instead of grinding it out for themselves.

Envy vs. Achievement

My husband and I often have discussions about how we notice when people envy what we and our successful entrepreneur friends have or when they say how they wish they could get the same results in their brand new fledgling businesses that we're getting after over 20 *years* in business. They complain and say how much they want our level of success, yet we observe and talk with them and they have *no idea* what it takes to get to where we are today. I don't know a single person who can build a six-figure business overnight, much less a multi-million dollar enterprise. Unless you happen upon an unexpected inheritance, win the lottery, or create a one-hit wonder product, it takes blood, sweat, tears, and a *lot* of laughing at yourself and picking yourself up off the floor of your own mistakes to make the magic happen and the dollars roll in.

> **TO THE TRUE ENTREPRENEUR, THERE IS NO SUCH THING AS "WORK"**

What it really takes is what my husband and I like to call "paying your dues." The late nights, the early mornings, the 3:00 a.m. discussions with your partner (if you're lucky enough to be with another entrepreneur that "gets" your weird timing for ideas) are all part of it. And while this may seem hard or even a little terrifying ("OMG I'm not sleeping as it is and now you want me to get up at 3:00 a.m. and go to WORK?!"), the fact is what it really takes to pay your dues, get your ass in that chair of productivity and make magical sparkly shit happen is for you to slap yourself upside the head with a mega mindset shift and realize that to the true entrepreneur there's **no such thing as work**. Work *is* life.

That's what makes the brainstorming at odd hours, the late nights, the early mornings, the putting off going out with friends in favor of getting that product launched all worth it. Because if you see it as "work" and it *feels* like work, you're royally screwed. The stress induced on your body just because your mind screams, "I'm working" will be much greater than if you come at your business with an attitude of play, enjoyment, and a "this is my awesome life" mindset. Without this playful mind shift you won't last more than the typical eight hours of work time in a day. You won't have the energy or drive to make your ideas become reality, because the "work" will drain your strength. Your ideas will remain just that—ideas—thoughts and dreams just waiting for the action that never comes. Your passion for that new idea will dry up... until you get *another* new idea. Then the cycle will repeat itself until you have dozens, if not hundreds, of "new" ideas partially started, collecting virtual dust on your hard drive, piling up as sticky-note sculptures on your desk, taunting you every time you see them. And the longer you wait to kick your own ass into gear the more likely some other entrepreneur will create it, and when you see what they've done you'll say, "See, I *knew* it was a good idea!"

That money and success could have been yours if you had gotten off your ass and taken action. While someone else producing your idea will validate it, the fact that *you* didn't create it will be another blow to your self-worth. And *that* is the Normalcy Trap most *want*repreneurs end up in. They love their ideas, they love the idea of more ideas, but they view making those ideas reality as "work," and the fear of having to work so much to make their dreams happen is strong enough to stop them often before they even start. And this is a crying shame, as it keeps tens of thousands of amazing products, services, and solutions hidden from the world.

IF YOU CAN'T VIEW THE PURSUIT OF YOUR DREAMS AS FUN, YOU'LL BURN OUT

If you can't view your passion, your entrepreneurial drive, and your pursuing of your dreams as fun, you'll burn out and blow up faster than a stick of dynamite with a quarter-inch fuse. Because while there will be stress (even good stress is still stress) and not every decision will be easy, the *fun*, joy, and excitement for what you're doing is what will keep you going. It's what will bribe you to keep your butt in that chair moving you closer to your goals. It's what kept me working on researching and ordering new store inventory until almost midnight one night when I had been fighting laryngitis for the previous two days. Because passion is powerful. Once you fully let your passion loose with permission to exponentially grow, it's an energetic force to be reckoned with. And it will feed your excitement, give you more energy, and motivate you to get whatever shit you need to get done to reach your ultimate goal, no matter how horrible you "feel" or how boring the work you need to do may seem to others.

Once you tap into that passion-energy, living in the Inner Realm of Asskickonomics becomes easier. Kicking your own ass into gear and motivating yourself isn't nearly as hard when you *want* to do the "work." When you're exited to see that goal come to fruition, when you channel that passion into energy to get it done, and when you're driven by the results you know you will see, you will reach those roots deep and tap into the source that will make you unstoppable! It's partial mindset shift and partial get-clear-on-your-goals that will help you grow those deep roots in the Inner Realm. So embrace fun, joy, and excitement and bribe yourself to take action on whatever difficult task is facing you right now... because as soon as you do you'll discover how much more powerful you are than you ever thought and you'll have tapped into a self-motivating secret most wantrepreneurs only dream of discovering: How to love what you do, especially when you're faced with your next challenge!

10

The Power of Your "WHY"

If you've read any business books before you've probably read a chapter on how important it is to find your "why." And it's true, because without a powerful enough reason to get out of bed in the morning you'll be severely tempted to stay snuggled under the comfortable, warm covers all day. It will be harder for you to get out of bed, much less pad over to your home office or get dressed and ready to get to work. Your why is the reason you do what you do to make money. It's the reason you don't rely on a boss somewhere to penalize you for being late to work. And unlike other "gurus" who preach about the power of your why and give examples of their noble whys being to take care of their kids or be there for their aging parents, I want to give you permission to have *any* why. Because having the why is more important than *what* that why is. You can listen to all the coaches and gurus in the world who talk about how important it is to have a why and still not claim yours, because maybe like I did for years, you feel yours isn't good enough, important enough, or noble enough. Common whys taught by gurus are your kids, schedule freedom, the ability to travel, a specific lifestyle... and it can and *will* change! There are many whys in the world and I would encourage you to try them all on. Think about every one of them and pay attention to your emotions as you do. When you feel that bubble of excitement (and even anxiety) deep in the pit of your stomach, *that's it*. It may not be your why forever, but it's a start and something for you to deep dive explore for a while.

YOUR FIRST WHY MAY NOT BE YOUR "WHY" FOREVER

Since I first started in business I've felt the pressure of finding my why. Every guru taught about it. Every keynote speaker at every conference I attended at least mentioned it; some even made their entire presentations about it. And I felt like a total business failure because I couldn't come up with a "good enough" why. Not having my clear why established became a Normalcy Trap for me of "shoulding" all over myself. After all, I *should* have a why. It *should* be a noble why, a good enough reason that when I shared it with others they would say, "Ohhhh yes, that's a great reason." My shoulds developed into coulds as I learned more about myself, my dreams and goals, and my personal vision for my future. (And just for the record, all of that continues to grow, expand, and change today.) I began my path while still in college when I started a stained glass art studio. Then I moved into photography and graphic design, which I did partly because I found I enjoyed it and partly because there was a lot more money in creating branding materials for companies than there was in creating stained glass. Then as that got old I started done-for-you publishing, ran multiple publishing companies, and at one point I actually started over 50 companies for other entrepreneurs. Then once again more money won as I realized teaching paid even more with less of a cap on how many people I could service through my done-for-you company. So I transitioned into teaching, following the money.

The Void Theory

Along my entrepreneurial journey I discovered something I call the Void Theory. I was constantly trying to fill voids in my life and sometimes they filled themselves... Because voids *must* be filled. It's a spiritual law. A practical example of this is when I moved from a townhouse with very little furniture to a larger 2500-square-foot home. After I moved in the house seemed really sparse. And less than two years later it was too crowded. Fast-forward about six years... My husband and I got new storage units when we didn't need them yet, just because they became available. And within a week they were full. We built a two-story four-car garage in our back yard to use as an art studio (and, well, garage... for one car anyway). And the week it was finished, we filled it. Finally, we added an addition onto our home with two beautiful dream offices, a guest suite, and a large living area and media room downstairs... and the day it was finished we—guess what—*filled* it. We didn't even know where all the "stuff" came from; it's like it just appeared! Can you relate? OK, so you've got the gist of the Void Theory.

I decided to take this Void Theory principle and apply it to my why: the why I beat myself up about for many years... *money.* That's right, my why was money. Money to give away, money to buy whatever I wanted, money to travel... money. And that didn't seem like a noble enough why, so my Normalcy Trap was to beat myself up about it. It took a conference where I saw Tamara Lowe speak to change my perspective from beating myself up about my why to embracing it and seeing an entirely new angle of it. She, like many other speakers I'd learned from over the years, said how impor-tant it was to have a why for all the same reasons I outlined at the beginning of this chapter. Then she said something that threw me back in my seat. She said that if your why was money, it was the noblest why of all. I was *shocked!* Here I was, about five years into putting myself down for having a non-noble-enough why, and Tamara was giving me *permission* not only to be OK with that why, but to *embrace* it!

And her explanation as to *why* the why of doing what I do for the money was a good thing gave me the freedom to get out of my Normalcy Trap and to embrace new ways of thinking, which ultimately led me to discover the Void Theory and apply it to my why. She made the point that *everything* is easier with money. It's easier to support your favorite charity, easier to enjoy a dinner out with your family, easier to relax on a family vacation, and easier to pay for unexpected car or house repairs when money isn't an issue and you have it in abundance. So I began to apply my Void Theory to my bank account. I mentally set a number that was my why number. Why do I implement that 3:00 a.m. idea? To keep my minimum in that bank account, that's why. I set a mental tag for one of my bank accounts that it should never fall below a specific number and if it did, the Void Theory would kick in and fill it back up again.

Because money naturally flows, I began to drain my account intentionally in ways that I knew would create the void. I gave

> # GIVE YOURSELF PERMISSION TO FULLY EMBRACE YOUR "WHY"

more to charities I supported (primarily my favorite, Toys for Tots). I helped out friends when they were in need. I surprised people by buying their coffee or groceries to pay it forward. I paid for lunch when I met up with another business friend, without her expecting me to. And you know what happened?

Not only did my account *grow* to the point of me having to set a new void level, but I began to have the time of my life in my business and recreational habits all because I finally gave myself permission to embrace my why!

How to Easily Discover Your "Why"

You may think your why is one of the first reasons that I gave and the fact is that your why can change and evolve. Just recently I discovered a new why and started to explore something I want to do that will cost much more money than I will make (at first). For the first time in my business life, my why has become something other than money... which I will leave for another book in this series ☺. Needless to say, finding and embracing your why is critical to your success as an entrepreneur. And allowing that why the freedom to change and grow as you evolve in your business life is equally important.

Here's an easy exercise to help you find your why:

⇨ Track your week. Write down every task you complete during the week.

⇨ Analyze those tasks. Which ones did you *love* and have fun doing? Which ones did you loathe and put off until the last minute? Which ones did you think about putting off, but didn't only due to a tight deadline?

⇨ Now write down your talents. What do you know you're good at? What lights you up inside? (Hint: If you're stuck on this, ask family and friends what they see as you talk about various parts of your day. Where have they seen you light up?)

⇨ And finally, answer this question: What do you value above all else? Is it the ability to drop everything and get a sick kid from school? Is it the freedom to travel around the world?

Is it the satisfaction of not having to say "no" to a charity due to lack of money?

As you do this activity you'll gain a clearer understanding of what your why is *for you*. It's different for every entrepreneur, though there are the common themes I mentioned earlier. And it's incredibly important because knowing your why is the number one motivator for Inner Realm success. It's the primary reason you do what you do even when you don't want to do it. It's the reason you call that client you've been dreading to tell some bad news. It's why you forgo that outing with friends to finish the book that's due to the editor the next day. It's the reason you push on when your business seems to be crumbling around you and you just want to quit. Your why is your biggest reason of all for everything, so take some time to discover it today. And don't beat yourself up if it's not what you expect it "should" be.

11

Get Clear on Your Goals

Without clearly set goals, your Inner Realm of Asskickonomics will remain untapped. I approach goal setting differently than most coaches, trainers, and consultants who instruct upon and have written books on the topic. While I agree that SMART goals are important, I think there's more to it than just goals being specific, measurable, attainable, realistic, and time-bound. The well-known and agreed-upon-by-all fact is that you have to have goals. Goal setting is not optional if you want to be focused and successful. A life without goals lets shit happen *to* you instead of *you* happening to your life. Not having any goals will leave you wide open to distraction. So we can all agree that goals are important. But do you *really* know what a goal is?

As you read that above paragraph you probably instantly nodded your head and thought, *Of course, a goal is something I set out to do, then do it,* or something similar. And while that's true to an extent, it's also true that some goals are more achievable than others. Some you'll complete quickly and easily. Then there will be some that you really want to complete, but for some reason you just never seem to be able to get ahead toward that finish line of completion. Many people view writing a book as one of these goals. The accepted statistic is that 80% of people want to write a book or think they have a book inside them and out of that 80% only 20% actually take action and see their work published. Having worked with and taught over 10,000 authors across a large chunk of the world, I can attest to the truth of that statistic.

Real Goals and Their Biggest Enemy

I believe that a real goal—one you can actually achieve—has several specific qualities. A real goal is practical. It's not pie-in-the-sky impossible, yet it will stretch your ideas of what *is* possible. It's reachable, yet challenging. A real goal is something you *know* you have it in you to achieve, yet maybe you can't explain how you know this fact. Well-meaning friends and family will challenge real goals. Let's take my friend Marie for an example. She always knew she wanted to be an entrepreneur. Yet when she actively took steps in that direction and set micro-goals to change her mindset and established real goals, friends and one close family member in particular gave her a hard time. After all, if you're an entrepreneur you don't have a steady income (or so the myth goes). A job is much "safer, more practical, and guaranteed income."

The disagreement over her desire for entrepreneurship and her family's desire for her to remain at home to take care of the kids or keep a regular job (both safe positions) strained her marriage to the point of divorce. And once her divorce was final she threw herself fully into entrepreneurship and hasn't looked back since. For those of us who are wired that way, being a full-time entrepreneur is a reachable, challenging, stretch-you-to-your-limits sort of goal. And when you set a deadline to a goal like that, shit gets real. You suddenly have a choice to make: Stay comfortable where you are

REAL GOALS ARE PRACTICAL

or move yourself up to play at another level. Having consistently "leveled up" dozens (maybe even hundreds at this point) of times over the years, I can personally attest to the fact that status quo and staying comfortable is *not* for the entrepreneur-wired individual.

Now while I personally believe these are the qualities of real goals, the fact remains that there's one singular enemy to achieving *any* goal and that is distraction. Just look at the number of car accidents every day in the United States alone. According to the Association for Safe International Road Travel, over 37,000 people die in the United States and an additional 2.35 million people are injured or disabled from car crashes... every *year*. Nearly one third of those people are between the ages of 16 and 20. And most accidents can be entirely avoided with *one* simple action: paying attention. Distractions are everywhere. They're on TV screens at major department stores as you're trying to get groceries for dinner. They're swimming around in your head as you walk through your house and notice a dozen things that need done like the dishes, laundry, and opening that pile of mail that's been sitting on your dining room table for the past week. And they're most obnoxiously in the notifications on your smartphone.

We live in the Age of Distraction where people use excuses like "life happened" as a reason for not seeing their goals through. While distractions can be toned down a little, such as by limiting the notifications you get on your phone, and sometimes they can be turned off by driving up in the mountains where there's no cell signal and no pile of laundry to command your attention, unless you want to be a hermit you can't live without them. They are *always* going to be there and they'll give you every excuse in the book not to finish what you start—not to complete your goal.

However, and this is a BIG however, the habit of entertaining your distractions is simply a mask for a much deeper-rooted issue. This issue could be perfectionism, procrastination, self-worth, fear of success or failure, fear of what other people may think, fear of repercussions with family or close friends... Whatever the issue, it's a powerful enough force to stop you in your tracks and leave your goal floating in the ideasphere just wishing and hoping it will happen. Occasionally your dream gets bold enough to show its awesome self to you again as it floats from your subconscious mind toward your conscious mind... just to slip back again. The most powerful example of this phenomenon I can give is the writing of the book you're holding in your hands right now.

Believe it or not, while I've written over 35 books (I lost count at 35), I've never written what I call a "heart-want" book until now. If you're one of those 80% who want to write a book, a heart-want book is that *one* book that's always on your mind, yet somehow seems impossible to write when you sit down to work on it. Oh, you get ideas all the time. They are plentiful as you jot them down on phone apps, sticky notes, and random notebooks you carry around like a good aspiring author would. But for some reason that heart-want book never goes from idea to action.

This book, *Asskickonomics*, was that way for me for almost three years. As I told the story in the *Introduction*, I got the idea two full years before I wrote a single chapter. Sure, I've written hundreds of thousands of words spread across multiple Kindle books, journals, coloring books, and training materials. But my heart-want book sat in my personal ideasphere just waiting for me to take action. It took a lot of personal growth, a lot of ass-kicking experiences (where I got my ass kicked), and a hard deadline to make me finally set my butt in the writing chair and take action. Writing short Kindle books was easy. In 2013 I even challenged myself and wrote 18 of them in 18 weeks which, honestly, I'd never do again, as that was over 117,000 words... in only 18 weeks! So why are heart-want books so hard to write? Why was *this book* so hard for me to write? Why are longer books in general harder to write than a huge series of shorties?

I have come to the conclusion that heart-want books, especially ones longer than a typical short 10,000-word how-to Kindle book, are hard for only *one reason:* we make them hard. Humans in general tend to overcomplicate tasks and make shit hard. This could be for many of the same reasons I've already outlined in this chapter. It could be because it's just the way we're wired. It could be because we're lazy and comfortable hanging out in our Normalcy Trap and don't want anything to change... and we know by completing our current biggest goal change *will* happen. But I'm here with some good news for you. With one commonly made-hard-yet-actually easy task, you can break free of your Normalcy Trap, tap into your Inner Realm of Asskickonomics, and kick major ass with *all* your goals for your life and business. Ready for that big secret?

Here it is... It's not really a secret. The one task that will change everything for you is to make a *decision*. Make a decision on how you're going to handle the influx of new product and business ideas. Make a decision to harness your most common distractions and put systems in place to handle new ones that will definitely come your way. Make a decision to stay *focused*. When you stop messing around with your goals and make a decision you actually gain resolve. You resolve yourself to lose that weight, finish that project, launch that new coaching program, etc. And resolve is much more powerful than simply getting clear on your goals or even setting them to begin with. Setting goals is easy. Tapping into the power of resolve to complete them is an entirely different matter altogether.

THE ONE TASK THAT WILL CHANGE EVERYTHING FOR YOU IS TO MAKE A DECISION

Now remember, you're going to mess up. Resolve is a powerhouse of the Inner Realm and it works well under pressure, deadlines, and the like. It also works best when paired with the accountability that more naturally occurs in the Upper Realm. And even with all the realms in place and fully tapped, "life" will happen and you'll screw up. You'll eat ice cream instead of a salad. You'll sleep in and miss that important meeting. You'll spend another hour watching sitcoms instead of working on your latest project (or writing your book… as I did… often… with *Asskickonomics*). It's in those times that you need to remember to implement the next most powerful task in accomplishing your goals, and that is *forgiveness*.

SET YOUR GOALS WITH FORGIVENESS FOR YOUR OWN SCREW-UPS

Set your goals with the knowledge of—and forgiveness for—your own screw-ups. Take responsibility and make the *choice* to acknowledge that it happened. Forgive yourself for getting sidetracked. Then pick your idea up again and run with it!

In some cases the curveballs life throws your way are completely unavoidable. I have an amazing, powerful, action-taking client who beat herself up (a little, I made her stop) for not completing her book goals this past year. However, the distractions life threw her way were in no way small or anything she could (or should) ignore. She lost family members, pets, and on top of all that, was diagnosed with cancer and had to undergo some serious operations. If *anyone* had a good reason to put off completing goals, it was her! When I read her long, apologetic email to me about how she didn't meet her goals, yet saw how upbeat she was about still completing them (this was two days after major surgery, mind you), I had to tell her what I'm about to tell you. It's OK. It's OK! It's totally OK to put a goal on hold in favor of healing your body, soul, and mind. It's OK to take time to heal, get treatment for whatever the issue is that comes up, and take a break from or pull back on your productivity for your goals. It's also totally OK to be OK with making that choice!

The important thing is to not stay in that place of despair and survival. When at all possible, yes, even with cancer, it's incredibly important to keep your mindset focused on taking care of yourself, which includes working on your goals as you're able. Sometimes an important goal is a powerful healing tool for whatever situation you may face. Because if you're passionate enough about it and stay focused toward reaching it, you *will* more likely have a chance to complete it. Your current goal may shift to becoming healthy again so you can devote the time necessary to complete your passion goal. And that's totally fine, as long as you don't lose sight of your that goal. So forgive yourself for the little missteps and the big life circumstances and notice when those things become excuses rather than good reasons why you're not completing your goals.

The Power of Habitual Goals

We all have habits. Humans are habitual creatures. Some habits are good, such as a routine of brushing your teeth every day. Some are not, such as smoking or consuming excessive amounts of alcohol. The cool thing about the Inner Realm is that by tapping into it and adding a little resolve, you can turn bad habits into good ones, which will significantly increase your productivity. I asked these questions in Chapter 4 and I'll ask them now again. Do you have a tendency to think the worst about situations that pop up in your life? Do you overuse the words "always" and "never?" Do you usually have more on your to-do list than you'll ever get done in a day... or week... or month? How about waiting until the last minute to do pretty much everything? Or feeling repeat disappointment in people, purchases, etc.?

These are all habits I've personally struggled with, and many of my entrepreneur friends have as well. They're common and they're all traps, especially if they become so much a part of your routine that you don't notice them anymore... effectively activating a Normalcy Trap.

The good news is you can train yourself to combat any of these self-destructive habits and it starts with something that sounds incredibly easy, yet isn't... because we make it hard. That first combatant is to think more highly of yourself. It's so incredibly important that you gain the ability to *see* yourself as who, what, and where you want to be. Do a visualization exercise where you close your eyes and think of your biggest passion goal. Hold it in your hands if it's tangible. *Feel* what you would feel if it were really there in front of you, accomplished. Tap into the emotion of successful completion and then open your eyes and re-enter the "real world." How did that make you feel?

Another key habit to create is to tell yourself every day that you're valuable and worthy of completing your goal. Any time you start to feel like the goal is too big for you or you're not good enough to complete, do the visualization exercise above and tap into the emotion of total satisfaction again. Emotion is such a powerful tool for setting new habits! If you can tie your goal in with a powerful, positive emotion, you'll build an association with that goal. Every time you think of working on it, dopamine will be released in your brain and you'll get such a good feeling about it that you'll want to work on it even more.

TELL YOURSELF EVERY DAY THAT YOU'RE VALUABLE AND WORTHY OF COMPLETING YOUR GOAL

Tapping into passion is the most powerful motivator in existence. And you can train your brain to respond with passion-driven emotion every time you think about that one thing you want to accomplish above all else.

Whenever you're stuck on your goals remember the Success Mind-Hack Formula from Chapter 4. It will help you to continue to build healthy mind-hacking habits that will set you up for faster and easier goal achievement, no matter what goal you set for yourself.

Goals vs. Resolutions vs. Lifestyle

Webster says a resolution is "The act of finding an answer or solution to a conflict, problem, etc.; the act of resolving something. The ability of a device to show an image clearly and with a lot of detail." While achieving goals can help you

YOU ARE NOT A PROBLEM OR BROKEN

see your path more clearly and it can certainly solve problems for you and for others, last I checked *you* are not a problem. *You* are not broken. Therefore, setting resolutions (which is different than having resolve) doesn't work. I can't name one out of dozens of my friends who have set New Year's Resolutions and actually saw them through. Resolutions imply that you have a problem and that problem is bad. However, problems are not always bad. Sometimes what we perceive as problems are simply life lessons, which can be hard, but they can turn out awesome.

In contrast to resolutions, Webster says a goal is "Something that you are trying to do or achieve." Now last time I checked, you do or achieve something *every* day, even if that something is simply to get out of bed. While that sounds good in theory, the fact is that goals and resolutions will not get you results unless you make them a part of your lifestyle. Here are some simple ways to do just that with your goals:

TAKE ONE SMALL STEP TOWARD YOUR BIG PASSION GOAL

Finish something. Anything. Even if it's a simple task; one step toward your big passion goal. If you habitually don't finish what you start, break free of your Normalcy Trap by finishing something and then celebrate it!

Apply your creativity. All human beings have some sort of creative talent, even if they don't think they do. My housekeeper told me she has no creative bones in her body. Yet I've seen the way she tackles my house and her problem-solving skills are incredible! Problem-solving skills don't exist without creativity.

Revisit an old project. Sometimes reviving an old project is the perfect way to gain clarity with your current ideas. I have often given my "stuck" writing clients an assignment outside their chosen genre. I've made non-fiction authors write a fiction piece related to the book they're "stuck" on. I've had fiction authors write a non-fiction article based on one part of their books. And in every case they've returned to me ready to leap back into the project on which they were initially stuck.

Appreciate yourself *every day* for who you are. Not for who you want to be or what you want to accomplish, but for who you *already are*. When you make this appreciation a habit you'll begin to see joy in everything that you do, whether you like to do it or not.

Quit chasing success and chase kindness, love, and joy instead. I love success just as much as the next entrepreneur. However, I've learned that focusing solely on success and money will only keep me from completing my passion project. Follow your passion and the money will come, as your excitement about it will be infectious!

Listen to the whispers of your heart and your emotions. When they creep up, especially if it's through tears, pay attention. Dive deep into the emotion and really *feel* it. Ask yourself why it's there, what triggered it, and how it relates to and will affect your goals.

Be present in the moment (this is so freaking hard sometimes) and be intentional with your decisions and actions. Put your big passion goal right in front of you (in your mind's eye is fine) and ask yourself this question any time an opportunity arises, "How will this new opportunity help me to complete my goal?" Intentions are the secret sauce to making positively impactful decisions toward your goals.

A lot of what I've shared so far (and yet to come) in this book is personal growth and development. You can make a lot of money and still remain an asshole. Or you can make a lot *more* money by building a solid foundation of growth for yourself. Be *you*. Love *you*. And rip apart that Normalcy Trap of self-deprivation so you can clear the fog around your goals and make your passion goal a reality!

12

Handle Your Distractions

Often called Shiny Object Syndrome or SOS, distractions are a prevalent part of our daily lives. How many times have you fought back road rage when driving across town? Or gotten upset that someone was looking at their phone instead of listening to you talk to them? The fact is people are distracted. And "shiny objects" are those distractions we choose to embrace that usually take us away from completing our passion goals.

However, SOS is OK in certain contexts. Human beings are designed to create. We're designed to be bombarded on all sides by stimuli, absorb our surroundings, then take what we absorb as inspiration to create something new. We're also curious by nature. It's how we grow and evolve. Without our innate curiosity, we humans wouldn't pave new pathways toward success, much less innovate something that has the power to change humankind forever. Do you think Steve Jobs wasn't curious about how he could fit 120,000,000 times the computing power of the Apollo computer that sent the Saturn V rocket to the moon in your pocket in the form of the iPhone 6? (Credit: Paul Ledak, former Vice President Microprocessor Development, 1982–2015.) It was curiosity that caused Jobs to launch the Apple-1 computer, the first in-home PC, which effectively changed the dynamics of home life in the United States forever. Today you'll be hard-pressed to find a home in the entire world without some sort of computing device assisting and distracting its inhabitants… all thanks to the curiosity of a few humans.

Without SOS, you may not have found this book. Without curiosity you wouldn't impulse buy anything, including that new healthy drink that helped you change your diet, lose weight, and feel sharper and more alert. Without the ability to be distracted, you wouldn't notice the little miracles that come your way. So SOS in its own right isn't necessarily evil, or bad, or even a negative. It's only when you use it as permission to create excuses for not staying focused on your passion goal that it becomes a problem and has the potential to grow into a habitual Normalcy Trap.

The SOS Enemy

Every day we're inundated with messages. From those annoying TV screens in the big box stores to the loud billboards flashing full-color images to the notifications on your phone, distractions are everywhere. If you feel you struggle with the negative side of SOS, the side that keeps you from accomplishing your goals and dreams, understand that marketing is *designed* to distract you! How else will people get your attention to buy their products if they don't turn your eyes away from something else to gaze upon their product's amazingness? Unless you know the personal reasons why you struggle with negative SOS and what easily distracts you, you'll never find a cure.

There are many reasons why you may be afflicted with negative SOS. One may be that you're dissatisfied with yourself or your current circumstances. Ever heard the popular phrase "the grass is always greener on the other side?" I personally love the line in the animated movie *Chicken Run* where the main rooster follows that thought up with, "And then you get there, and it's brown... and prickly." His point was that if you're continuously seeking opportunity for fulfillment elsewhere, you'll miss the incredible opportunities already sitting in your lap. And that incredible opportunity is the completion of your current passion project.

Another reason you may fight SOS is indecision. To be honest, indecision drives me absolutely nuts. In fact during a recent trip to Target I was standing in an unusually long line with a fairly full cart. A new cashier opened a line and called out that she was ready for customers. I waved on a couple of people who were in the same position as me in the next line, as they only had a few items. It took them literally over 15 seconds to decide whether they even *wanted* to go to the new cashier or continue to wait... and that drove me nuts so I shook my head, muttered "your loss" under my breath and dashed to that line. I have places to go, people to see, and goals to accomplish. I don't have time to wait around on the indecisiveness of others. Their why for how they should spend their time was either nonexistent or not nearly as strong as mine, so they forfeited their place in line and I got through, checked out, and on my way a good 15 minutes in front of them. This gave me 15 more minutes that I could spend writing down ideas, taking action on a project, getting to my next destination faster... an infinite number of possibilities. Instead of knowing their goals and taking action, those people wasted their 15 minutes waiting in a line when they could have jumped to the front of it.

> **LOOK FOR THE INCREDIBLE OPPORTUNITY THAT IS ALREADY SITTING IN YOUR LAP**

Some people lack discipline and follow-through and while they may start out with good intentions, they just don't seem to have the resolve it takes to stay "butt-in-chair" until a project is finished. Instead, their good intentions end up as false hopes for what's practical (remember the power of realistic goals from the last chapter?) and their overwhelming desire for a magic button that will make their dreams come easier becomes such a stronghold they jump on any new shiny object that promises success.

The reason why the negative side of SOS affects most human beings is because we're still searching for what resonates with us. This search fuels indecision, dissatisfaction, and a lack of discipline. When "shit hits the fan" and we hit a wall that makes something hard to accomplish, we get tired, distracted by that shiny new marketing email, and jump into the next opportunity only to repeat this same scenario over and over again with each new wall we smack ourselves into. In contrast, when you find that one passionate thing that pushes all your happy buttons and gives you joy, staying focused becomes easy. Unfortunately, most humans live their entire lives in search of that one passion, which takes them from one shiny object to another in hopes that the next new "squirrel" will provide desperately sought-after answers.

Destroy SOS

There are several traits successful entrepreneurs possess that effectively destroy SOS. The first is something I've already mentioned in this book several times and that is to be the best *you* that you can be. Not the best internet marketer, not the best employer, not even the best mom or dad. But the best *you*. I said it before and I'll say it again... when you strip away everything you identify yourself *as* you're left with only *one thing*: You. The purest, most raw, essence of human *you*. Embrace that *you* and love it. Be honest with yourself. Know your strengths and skills and focus to hone them to be even better. Outsource your weaknesses. And know your values. How does what you value shape your decisions and who you have become? I personally highly value integrity. You may think that's a great value to have, yet

BE THE BEST YOU THAT YOU CAN BE

it often gets in my way as I become so hard on myself when I get distracted that I start "shoulding" all over myself because I'm not doing what I "should" be doing.

Once you're clear on your values and know what your core passion is, give yourself permission to tune out anything that doesn't align with your goals. This will help you stay disciplined and focused to finish what you start. And when you reach a limit of your own knowledge or skill, push a little farther. Recognize what's realistic for you to accomplish and surprise yourself with what you can achieve! When you push your limitations, assemble anything you need to stay on task with your goals. These may be tools, time, training courses, etc. Just make sure everything you assemble in your success toolbox is in line with your primary objective and goal.

Remember that new ideas will continuously bombard you no matter how focused or driven you may be. Capture those ideas in a way that works for you then move on to the next task on your passion goal to-do list. You may carry around a notebook or jot down your ideas in Evernote on your phone. However you handle the influx of new ideas, if they're not related to your current passion project get them out of your head and tucked away some-where safe so they stop pestering you. Use the old "out of sight, out of mind" adage to your advantage!

Shiny objects often present themselves when you're struggling with a personal objection to completing your goal. Think about this... when was the last time you were working on your passion project and checked your email for something that you thought would help you with it, then ended up reading a well-meaning marketing email from someone, clicked the link in the email, and ended up buying another product or training course completely unrelated to the project you're currently working on that sent you searching your email in the first place? Yes, that was pretty specific and I know it happens because I do it too! No human is immune to SOS... which is why if you're subconsciously uncomfortable with something related to your project you'll unintentionally seek out distractions that will keep that project from completion. Most of the time these SOS distractions show up when you have a self-worth issue to deal with. You may not recognize it as that at first, but think about that last time you were working on something you're passionate about, then your mind started to spin and you got stuck because you went hunting for something else that would make money faster, get to market faster, or something else suddenly just became more interesting.

If you have a habit of continually starting multiple projects and never actually seeing any of them completed, marketed, and in customer's hands, it's time for you to ask yourself the hard question, "What am I objecting to about getting this project done?" You may not be happy with what you discover and that's all part of growing into your full potential as a creative human being.

> **ASK YOURSELF WHAT IS REALLY KEEPING YOU FROM GETTING YOUR PASSION PROJECT DONE**

Finally, the number one way to destroy SOS forever is to maintain accountability with yourself and others. You knew this was going to come up, right? After all, it's a common theme throughout this book. Until you learn how to maintain your focus by kicking your own ass and allowing others a kick or two here and there also, you'll jump from half-finished project to half-finished project, never completing a damn thing. And that's the biggest disservice you can do for yourself and the world as it hides your brilliance and keeps solutions from others who are actively seeking them out.

Five SOS-Busting Questions

Like I said at the beginning of this chapter, SOS isn't necessarily a negative. Sometimes it allows us to find helpful tools and resources that make our lives and businesses easier. But how do you know if it's a positive or negative shiny object? Simply ask yourself these five questions any time you're presented with a new tool, training course, business opportunity, etc.:

Do I really *have the time, money, ability, and focus to do this now?*

If what you're contemplating investing your time, energy, and money into isn't something that can help you reach your current goals, the likelihood of you ever using it is slim to none. I and other marketers often use copy like this while marketing my training courses: "Even if you don't plan to use this now, grab it at this reduced price so you'll have it when you're ready for it!" And while I may be shooting my own business in the foot by daring to say this, the fact is this is only marketing copy used to get indecisive buyers to open their wallets. Those opportunities are rarely lost forever (with the exception of product retirement sales) and when you're ready for it, it will be available to you. It's true that it may cost you a little more in the future, but the fact is it will cost you a *lot* more if you spend money on it and never use it vs. if you save your time, energy, and money for when you actually *will* use it.

Does this get me closer to my goal?

This question is super simple. If the answer is a resounding "yes!" then get it. If it's a maybe or a no, don't.

Why *do I want or need to do this* now?

This question can be a tough one as it may bring up the personal objection you have to completing your next goal. There's a difference between just being curious and having money to burn on something you may or may not end up using right now and the perfect opportunity presenting itself right when you need it. If you know it will help you right *now* and you have a good reason why you want it, then snatch it up.

What need does doing this thing or buying this XYZ really *fill?*

Again, this can be a tough question as it may make you uncomfortable. If you start analyzing your needs and wants you may discover something about yourself you don't want to see: voids you're trying to fill with "stuff" because of a loss or some other tragedy, an overcompensation for how you really feel about yourself... the needs that you're trying to fill can go on and on.

What's the worst that could happen if I do not *take action on this?*

Believe it or not, this is the most freeing question of all. This is the question that will answer whether it's a "life or death" investment of your time, energy, and money. If the worst thing that could happen isn't that bad, like missing out on saving $20, then it's not nearly as bad as never finishing your passion project or accomplishing your goals before you die.

The bottom line is unless the shiny objects you want to embrace lay a foundation and create a structure that will build and support your ultimate vision, they're best left in Shinyville to distract someone else. Leave them be and expect the positive shiny objects to appear right when you need them. Start to expect everything that comes your way to align with your passion and you'll be surprised how much you'll attract those positive shiny objects instead of continuously seeking treatment for the negative effects of SOS. Peter Dinklage (Tyrion Lannister from *Game of Thrones*) said in an inspirational speech, "Don't bother telling the world you are ready. Show it. Do it." Action is an incredible force. When taken even if you're not fully ready, solutions to your blocks will show up. You've heard the phrase, "when the student is ready, the teacher appears"? The same principle is true here. When you set your plans in motion, set goals, and take steps toward achieving those goals, everything you need to accomplish them will appear. It's up to you to pick up that power tool of passion and use it to build your dream... or to continue trying to chisel away at your ultimate goal with a toothpick.

EXPECT EVERYTHING THAT COMES YOUR WAY TO ALIGN WITH YOUR PASSION

13

The Biggest Distraction

The biggest distraction you'll ever face to achieving your passion goal is not lack of time, energy, or money. Rather it cloaks itself as one of these more common excuses. The *real* distraction is self-sabotage. Self-sabotage often shows up in your thoughts and little whispers you tell yourself. In fact it may be such the norm for you that until it's pointed out that you do it, it will be an unrecognized Normalcy Trap.

Let me ask you something... Have you ever found yourself thinking or saying any of these questions or phrases out loud?

⇨ "No matter what I do I just can't seem to get ahead."

⇨ "I keep making the same mistakes over and over and..."

⇨ "Last month was good, but this month I have to start over."

⇨ "She has XYZ... She's doing XYZ. I could totally do that better. But I haven't yet."

⇨ "I keep forgetting about..."

⇨ "It is what it is."

⇨ "I'll be happy when XYZ happens."

⇨ "I should have..."

Do You "Should" on Yourself?

I've mentioned "shoulding" on yourself a lot because that final phrase in the list above is one of the most dangerous Normalcy Trap habits you can have. "Shoulding" on yourself makes you lesser than. It also gives you permission to give up. It puts you in the position of never being good enough. And if you're consistently never good enough, you'll keep putting off your *big* goals for fear they won't be perfect enough to accomplish anyway. It's time to *quit shoulding on yourself!*

OFTEN WE DON'T REALIZE SELF-SABOTAGE IS HAPPENING UNTIL AFTER IT'S HAPPENED

Now you may say, "But I don't think I really self-sabotage. I mean, I'm quite successful. In fact look what I've accomplished!" Here's why self-sabotage is so dangerous... because most of the time we don't realize it's happening until *after* it's happened. It often manifests itself in repeated scenarios. For example, I personally have an issue with "tech" going bad. Whether it's a site update that makes my entire webpage editor disappear or recurring issues with our payment processors, it seems tech is always having one issue or another. I've had to explore some depths inside me that led to these tech issues being a manifestation of my own self-sabotage. And guess what? Once I targeted those issues (which seemed entirely unrelated, by the way), my tech issues stopped being so frequent!

Another way self-sabotage shows up for many entrepreneurs is having really good income months followed by horrible ones. In their book *Driven*, Douglas Brackmann and Randy Kelley talk about how driven entrepreneurs often create scenarios of scarcity so that they can then swoop in, create a new product, and instantly become the hero. Entrepreneurs are famous for always wanting to play the hero of their business, especially uber successful ones! In fact Walt Disney himself had this habit as he said himself, "I function better when things are going badly than when they're as smooth as whipped cream." He made this habit of heroism when "things went badly" work for him in building the foundations of his empire. And imagine how much less stressful it would have been if he'd recognized his Normalcy Trap of creating scarcity and playing the hero and took more effective action to plan!

Both of the above scenarios contribute to a habit you may have noticed in yourself: Putting yourself down. "If I could only..." and "I always do that!" are common phrases often spoken by entrepreneurs who hold such high standards for themselves they create an environment in which it's nearly impossible to reach those standards. When those tech issues kept coming up I said things like, "If I could only learn this for myself" or "I always freak out when these tech issues happen!" And worse yet, until you're consciously aware of what's being spoken inside your head these utterances usually happen without you even noticing it. They're so habitual they're almost a part of you. And as long as they remain a habit you will keep hitting that ceiling where the possibility of your dreams is just outside the skylight.

The first step to breaking through that glass ceiling into the realm of possibility is to pay attention to when you use these phrases. You can begin to notice them by setting trigger words for yourself. Absolutes such as "always," "never," "nobody," and "everyone" are trigger words to let you know something's up and you're dangerously close to the panic zone of self-sabotage. Notice the cycle of when these words creep up. There's *always* a cycle. Is it hormone-driven? Is it when you're sleep deprived? Is it when you've had an incredibly stressful week and haven't taken any time for yourself?

Your emotions are also a key telltale that something's not right in your Inner Realm. Pay attention to the tension in your shoulders, the number of times you sigh, your frustration at situations, and your words. All those things will help you set triggers for yourself so you can consciously decide whether you want to pull yourself out of the self-sabotage danger zone or dip your toe in it for a while. By giving yourself the power of *choice* in those situations you keep your power. You can choose to let off some steam, be angry, and vent. What's important is that you recognize that as your *choice*, not as a default you keep finding yourself going to.

Your closest family and friends will also be able to help you notice when things are amiss. While this brings the Upper and Lower Realms into the mix, that's ultimately where the power lies in Asskickonomics. By encouraging those around you to hold you accountable to what you say, when you put yourself down, how you react to the unexpected, etc., you're allowing all three realms simultaneously to play in harmony together. Ask those close to you to notice and call out (in love) when they see you heading down that spiral.

The Power of Gratitude

I've mentioned it before and it's important enough to mention again. Gratitude is the most powerful antidote to self-sabotage in existence! When my husband Tony went through his divorce, his dad died, his dog died, he lost his home, and he was literally eating off a card table in an empty apartment. His business had just reached success, yet his life had become a classic country song. After asking, "Why is this happening to me?" over and over and over again, he finally shut up and listened. And the message he received is one he's drilled into every human being that will listen ever since. "Stop focusing on what you don't have and be thankful for what you do have." It was in that moment he became brutally honest with himself and recognized that he was trying to do everything he could to find a reason to *not* find a solution to his problems. He was so focused on self-preservation that he failed to see what was right in front of his face.

Thus began his long journey of discovery as to what gratitude really means. It seems like such a simple thing, yet its meaning and impact are so deep he's still getting clarity on how it applies to different areas of his life today.

STOP FOCUSING ON WHAT YOU DON'T HAVE AND GIVE THANKS FOR WHAT YOU DO HAVE

You can't be on very many of his webinars before you hear him say something like, "Stop focusing on what you don't have, what's not working, how you 'suck'... and stay in a place of gratitude and give thanks for what you *do* have." It's become his mantra, his mission statement, and in living with him and seeing how it plays out daily in our lives, it's become mine too.

Sometimes it's incredibly hard to see the "silver lining." In fact just the other day one of my students said to me, "I love how you always see opportunity." What she did not see was my emotional breakdown just an hour prior on the phone with my coach. She didn't see the tears or hear the sobs. And she didn't know they were loud enough that when my husband (who was upstairs in another section of the house) later asked, "Were you crying on the phone with your coach? I thought I heard something." All of us have those breakdown moments. That's where forgiveness and allowing yourself to be an emotional human being (and yes, sometimes an emotional wreck) for at least a few minutes comes into play. The important thing is to not stay there, as that's when it leads to self-sabotage and it will distract you from your true purpose in life and for your business. The only way to escape that spiral of depression is with gratitude.

Once you make it a habit to notice and be thankful for what you have, anxiety, anger, depression, and mood swings will decrease. They may disappear altogether. Your relationships may change as you are suddenly aware that the company you used to keep was feeding your self-sabotage rather than supporting you to grow beyond it. Sometimes ties must be severed for you to grow or your business *will* stagnate and eventually die.

You'll also notice how your desire for better health, more money, and the ability to truly be yourself are increased. Your income *will* change as money is a common manifestation of self-sabotage. You'll lack it when you're sabotaging; you'll be more flush when you aren't.

Step In and Step Out

One way to get out of a Normalcy Trap of self-sabotage is to journal. Morning Pages, as explained in *The Artist's Way*, is a great way to get all those tumbling thoughts out of your head first thing in the morning so you can be on your way to greatness in your business. Simply keep a journal beside your bed and first thing in the morning when you wake up write down *every* thought spiraling in your head, no matter what that thought may be. It may even start with something like, "I don't have any thoughts. I'm not awake yet." And that's

> **IT'S TIME FOR YOU TO BOLDLY BE THE YOU THAT'S BEEN HIDDEN INSIDE**

OK! The important thing is to get anything out that's stuck there, keeping you from being able to focus on what's necessary for your success. That may be an overwhelming to-do list or thoughts that you're overwhelmed. It doesn't matter *what* you write, but *that* you write.

It's time for you boldly to be the YOU that's been hidden inside underneath a cloak of self-sabotage. It's time for you to pay attention. Start to notice your patterns. Notice your emotions. If you feel the spiral, make the conscious choice to experience the emotion. Dive deep, explore, and ask tough questions of yourself. Ask yourself where this feeling is coming from. Did something happen that triggered it? Has it happened before? Is this a pattern? Noticing is only half the equation; taking action is the other half. Change is scary. It freaks us out. And it's *necessary* to *truly LIVE!* Without your willingness to do what it takes to change you'll remain where you are and you'll stagnate in your Normalcy Trap of self-sabotage.

As you do these exercises, pay attention to your progress. Give yourself some benchmarks and celebrate and give thanks for your successes. Celebrate *every* win! You're awesome and you're meant to touch those you come into contact with in your business with the greatness that's inside of you. So smile at your brilliance and own your awesomeness. You don't need to self-sabotage to get what you want or need. You have permission to be fully *you* and to rock your business!

14

Workaholics Anonymous

As you sink your roots of success deeper into the Inner Realm and get clear on your focus, your drive and passion will demand most of your attention and time. People who don't understand what you're doing and why you're doing it will continually pull at you to stay comfortable with them. To keep doing less than you know you can accomplish. Not to go for that thing that will set you apart from them once you reach it.

The Workaholics Anonymous Phenomenon

I've seen it develop so many times. You've finally stepped into your role as an entrepreneur and you get super excited about your new venture. That passion, energy, and drive we explored in earlier chapters is revving up to full force. You're exploring the fertile entrepreneurial earth around you, ready to sink those roots in deep and grow tall toward your dreams. Then you get invited to go out with your "friends" and as soon as you start talking about your new venture or your excitement starts to show, or you start using any kind of unrecognizable-to-them "business" language, your "friends" give you that gut-wrenching look of non-understanding and jokingly call you a "workaholic." You're taken aback by this idea. After all you're finally living into your passion which is anything *but* work, right? And how could they not encourage and support you and be interested in what you're creating? After all, they're your *friends.*

THE MORE YOU PURSUE YOUR DREAMS, THE MORE YOU'LL SET BOUNDARIES ON YOUR TIME

Suddenly you realize that they can't comprehend what you're talking about because they're simply not wired like you, and it slowly sinks in that ultimately you may be faced with the choice between your friends and your dreams. Because the more you pursue your dreams, the more you'll set boundaries on your time (remember Chapter 6) and the more distant your "friends" will become as they just can't wrap their heads around why this "business thing" is so important to you. And because humans are designed for community, usually your friends will win. Your new business venture idea will fall by the wayside, your roots will stop growing and shrivel up, and you'll have that constant back-of-the-mind nagging that something isn't complete in your life... that you have more to accomplish... that you're meant for more than just drinking on the weekends and fulfilling your boring duties at your run-of-the-mill-soul-sucking day job... and you wake up every morning feeling like depression is closer and closer to your door.

Sound familiar? If you haven't encountered it yet, you probably will. There will come a point in time when you'll be faced with that decision to pursue your dreams and surround yourself with people who "get" it or stay where you're at. Either way you may end up coming to the point of owning your decision to become a "workaholic" and have to discover connections to new friends. What's interesting to me is how many of these "friends" I've had who were envious of my business accomplishments, yet who didn't envy how much I "work." Several years ago I was sitting in a waiting area for a martial arts class next to a fellow adult karate student, who I wouldn't necessarily call a friend, but was enough of an acquaintance that I felt comfortable talking to him. In response to his question about weekend plans, I told him about how excited I was to escape the cold the next week and go for a cruise in the Caribbean.

While this would have been my third cruise, I was mostly excited to be getting away... to work. It was a marketing event cruise where I'd be in sessions during each day at sea, master-minding at dinner every evening, and working on my business via sucky boat Wi-Fi. And it all sounded glorious. The student next to me only heard "cruise," immediately responded with a scowl and said, "Must be nice." If you haven't gotten the "must be nice" reaction from someone yet, give it time. It will come.

In this case, I wasn't fully equipped for a non-bitter reply as I'd gotten tired of hearing lazy people's jealous responses to exciting things I was doing. So I responded with a bit of a tirade, which I'm neither proud of nor regretful of saying. I said, "What you don't realize is this is a *work* cruise. Yeah, I get to get away. But I'm mostly excited because I get to focus on growing my business and connecting with new people in my field. Also, I worked my butt off seven days a week for four *years* straight just so I could get my business to the point that it could sustain me for four *days'* worth of true vacation... and I haven't had a real vacation in over two years. So don't give me that 'must be nice' crap when you haven't seen the dues I've paid to get where I am today." Yeah, it may have been a bit much, but as he had also seen me drop guys twice my size in my karate classes, his response was kind of price-less when he leaned back in his chair, his eyes went wide, and he said, "Remind me *never* to make you angry." It was in that moment that I was reminded why I refuse to hang out with people of his limiting beliefs mindset.

"Workaholics" and Friends

The phrase "You're the average of the five people you spend the most time with" is one of the deepest, truest sayings in existence. It's not a matter of *if* you will ever face the difficult decision to end relationships in favor of your dream, but *when*. Steve Kamb, founder of Nerd Fitness and author of *Level Up Your Life*, initially spent most of his off-day-job time playing video games, partying, and traveling for a long-distance relationship. It was only when his computer's hard drive fried that he was faced with the stark reality of working on his dream *or* playing video games and getting drunk. At first he decided to build his business so he could quit his job and be location independent, freeing up time for his girlfriend. Then a series of events happened and he realized he also needed to "level up" his friends. In his words: "I was then faced with a really difficult decision regarding my relationship, which I decided to end. I didn't know at the time if I was making the right decision, but something in my gut told me I was. It seems so obvious now, looking back, but if you've ever struggled to get out of a relationship that isn't quite right, you know it can feel like a sacrifice" (*Level Up Your Life*, Chapter 20, p. 223).

If you're building a business alongside your normal day job and life, you already know the time and energy fledgling businesses

> **YOU ARE THE AVERAGE OF THE FIVE PEOPLE YOU SPEND THE MOST TIME WITH**

require. I started my publishing business in 2003 while also working several part-time jobs. The late nights, early mornings, and weekends I spent working on my business helped it morph and grow into a half-million-dollar publishing and training empire and it's continuing to grow beyond publishing today. I didn't have much time for hanging out with friends and usually if I went out it was to networking events and meetups. I learned early on that if I wanted to be full-time with my own company and get to where I am today with multiple businesses, investment companies, and employees, I had to sacrifice some events and ties with specific types of people in favor of my dream. It wasn't easy, but I agreed with what I've noticed in every other entrepreneur I've ever studied... the tenacity that is necessary to win at this game we call business... and the power of true friends who "get" your "workaholism" and gladly support you within it.

Is it REALLY "Workaholic"?

If you Google the term "workaholic," one of the first results you'll get is a blog post from December 15, 2011, on Psychology Today by Barbara Killinger PhD that starts with, "Workaholism is a soul-destroying addiction that changes people's personality and the values they live by." Whoa. The list that followed that definition of answers to "questions people ask" are almost humorous. They would be hilarious if not for the fact that common society has bought into this definition of the "disease" hook, line, and sinker. Because if you love what you do and love work, something *must* be wrong with you. And if you discover what you want to do with your life in the form of your new business, those who are jealous of your success or just don't understand will claim that you must be ill and have the workaholism disease. In fact under the question "Is workaholism a disease?" is another answer from a blog post dated July 18, 2013, on Psychology Today by Brad

Klontz PsyD, CFP, "Workaholism is a family disease often passed down from parent to child. Workaholics use work to cope with emotional discomfort and feelings of inadequacy. They get adrenaline highs from work binges and then crash from exhaustion, resulting in periods of irritability, low self-esteem, anxiety and depression." WOW! Makes me glad I'm not a psychologist with such a negative view of the work world.

Speaking as a self-proclaimed "workaholic" I can attest to the fact the above is *not* true… for the driven entrepreneur. While my ex-husband was quick to point out, "You're happiest when you're going away to a business event," there was a reason for that. He was right. I *was* happiest when I was around others who understood me, who didn't think I was weird for wanting to brainstorm marketing ideas until 2:00 a.m., and who woke up with those harebrained ideas at 3:00 a.m. on a regular basis themselves. I was *un*happy when I was forced to conform to be someone I wasn't, to ignore my inner drive, and to stay in a position where I couldn't rise to my full potential as a business woman. It got to the point where "workaholic" was thrown around my home like the derogatory term that Google says it should be, directed at me and my increasing happiness with my… work. And in case you skimmed past it above, that was my EX-husband. My amazing husband today is an entrepreneur himself and the biggest problem we have is one of us being awake enough at 4:00 a.m. to listen to the big idea the other got and has already been mulling over the details of for the past hour.

> **WHEN YOU LOVE WHAT YOU DO, THERE'S NO SUCH THING AS WORK-LIFE BALANCE**

It's so sad that society has taught people to hate their jobs even to the point of coining the term, "soul-sucking day job." As an employer it saddens me to hear anyone talk about their job in that way. I wish everyone loved what they do as much as I do. And when you love what you do there's no such thing as work-life balance. Instead it's work, it's life, and it's already balanced, because you're living into the full potential of who you're *meant* to be, 24/7. While I agree some people may be "addicted" to work, I personally believe what the world views as an addiction is simply an outward indication of something inwardly wrong, whether it be an unhappy home life, dissatisfaction with their choices, etc. If workaholism truly is an addiction to cover up a deeper problem, often it will be accompanied by other addictions such as gambling or alcoholism.

In contrast, entrepreneurs who *love* what they do so much that they can be found late at night glued to their computer screen typing away on a manuscript at 75 words-per-minute aren't necessarily workaholics. Instead they're simply people who understand that when the passion, energy, and ideas align, it's time to take action, and the clock means nothing to them. True entrepreneurs still binge watch their favorite shows, they still take walks in nature to clear their heads, and they still hang out with friends. What's different is *when* they do these things, how often they do them, and what friends they choose to hang out with.

So while your "friends" may call you a workaholic, keep in mind that if you love what you do so much it doesn't feel like work, if it energizes you rather than drains you of energy, if you wake up jazzed and excited and just can't *wait* to take action on that idea, even if that means you're still in pajamas past lunch, all this means is that you're an entrepreneur who loves what you do, not that you have some disease or something is wrong with you.

15

The Lower Realm

The Lower Realm of Asskickonomics is the most ignored realm of all, yet it's the most critical to your personal (which spills over into professional) success. If you are in a position of authority over others you're in their Upper Realm, which puts them in your Lower Realm. Chances are you're in the Upper Realm in relationship to others, especially in your business. These may be virtual assistants (VAs), employees, independent contractors, temporary hires, interns, etc. At the time of this writing, my husband and I have eight employees for our multiple retail businesses with more new hires and interns about to start in a few months as we have plans to open more new stores. To them I'm "the boss." I'm the one they come to for assignments, permission for time off, and if they have any questions or concerns about a project I'm the one they look to for the answers. I'm responsible to pay attention to what's affecting their work quality and address it. Sometimes this task ends up being something my husband and I help them address in their personal lives, which is spilling over and affecting the quality of their work lives. We are in their Upper Realm and they're in our Lower Realm, as we tell them what to do and they look to us for guidance.

Accountability to the Accountable

And while they're accountable to get their work done, I'm also accountable to them. I hold levels of responsibility they don't have the ability to access. If we're working on a new project, they know they have the freedom to voice their opinions and ideas even if I may disagree, because I've intentionally created the safe environment that allows them to do so. In Chapter 3 of his book *Originals*, *New York Times* bestselling author Adam Grant tells the story of mid-level manager Donna Dubinsky at Apple who decided to go head to head with her bosses and even the owner of the company, Steve Jobs himself, and stand her ground on an issue of distribution. At first her voice was overruled; then when given the opportunity to stand up for what she felt was right for the company, employees, and most of all, the customers, she put her own job on the line in an ultimatum that if she couldn't come up with a better solution for their distribution issues within 30 days than what Steve Jobs himself had already presented and begun to put in motion, she would leave the company. It was a huge risk and when her appeal was granted, she presented a proposal that was ground-breaking in the computer distribution industry and that effectively changed the course of how they serviced customers. What may have seemed like a losing battle to other employees turned into a promotion and ultimately a program developed to reward one person every year who challenged a decision Jobs made. And Steve Jobs's response to these challenges from those in his Lower Realm? He promoted every one of them.

If you're in the Upper Realm to others—be it team members, a VA, employee, or even your housekeeper—magic happens when you pay attention to those under you and *give them permission* to hold *you* accountable. If you respond with grace and seriously consider their suggestions rather than take the defensive position of "my way or the highway" every time they have an idea, you'll discover a whole awesome company culture that will enable your business to thrive and grow.

Our employees often come to me with ideas to solve problems they've noticed at our toy store. From putting up a sign to leave dogs outside after one peed all over our original 1800s wood floors and got into children's toys thinking they were his to creating silly emojis within our company communication system to foster growth and a fun work atmosphere, because of the safe environment we've created for them to do so, the ideas are always flowing and often take us pleasantly by surprise as to their ingenuity and effectiveness.

Don't get me wrong: it's not always easy. There have been times I've had intense discussions late into the night with my husband about one or more of our employees and how we're to handle unique situations with them, especially if they take action on their ideas without thinking them through or running them past us first. In these cases I have to be OK with losing the time in the conversation that follows, because I'm the one who created the safe environment for them to share ideas to begin with. And that's not easy for me to admit! Being in a position of authority can be as scary as it is rewarding. And honestly, it's not for everyone. If you want your business to grow beyond what you can provide for your own family and "just get by," then you need to remain open to inhabiting the Upper Realm and

> # IT'S IMPORTANT TO CREATE A SAFE ENVIRONMENT FOR THOSE IN YOUR LOWER REALM TO SHARE IDEAS, ENERGY, AND RESOURCES

tapping into the genius your Lower Realm can offer you... and ultimately you must be OK with what it can cost you in time, energy, and resources.

The Challenge

Employees or VAs may develop a habit of continually pushing your boundaries, monopolizing your time, and needing to be micromanaged. Part of inhabiting their Upper Realm is knowing when to call it quits and have the tough conversation with them and to empower them to make their own decisions, or, better yet, not to present a problem unless they have also come up with a solution. I've had the micromanaging issue with three people who worked for me and were in my Lower Realm. While I encouraged each of them to hold me accountable, I also demanded the same from them. In all three cases they didn't hold up their end of accountability so it fell on my shoulders to take the tough responsibility of the Upper Realm and to hold them accountable for their non-action.

> **YOU MAY HAVE TO HOLD THE LOWER REALM ACCOUNTABLE FOR THEIR NON-ACTION**

In two of the above cases, I ultimately had to let the employees go. Both were angry. Both didn't understand how I could "be so mean." And both, within a couple of weeks, came back to me and said I was right about them. One went on to pursue the dream she had given up years before of becoming a nurse. The other got presented the opportunity of a lifetime with a paid-for degree, paid internship, and high-paying job waiting for her at the end of the two-year degree program.

She's at the top of her class and is thriving. I'd like to think that both of them are where they are today *because* I was willing to take the responsibility of doing the hard thing and setting them free. If I hadn't done that, they'd still be struggling along trying to do the jobs they weren't suited for and I would still resent having to micromanage them.

Not having kids myself (who are also in your Lower Realm, by the way), I finally understood the phrase my mother always used to say when she disciplined me: "This is going to hurt me more than it hurts you." Letting team members go, especially when you see and believe in their potential, is the most difficult thing I've ever done. And as "the boss" it falls on my shoulders to do this any time it becomes an issue. Sometimes by cutting loose those in your Lower Realm you actually enable and propel them forward to accomplish *their* lifelong goals and dreams. Being in your Lower Realm may actually be what's been holding them back!

The Reward

The third situation of micromanagement has yet to play out fully as I'm writing this manuscript. In her performance review we gave her a plan she had to follow. And while for the most part she's been following it, it's also become clear there are some areas in which she excels and some in which she struggles. As you develop your Lower Realm, an important thing to be aware of is that some people aren't willing to acknowledge their weaknesses. They think they can do it all and they want nothing more than to please you. The fact is you may not even know what they're incapable of until you give them a task in which they fail miserably, and that is *your* responsibility, not theirs.

In the case of this employee, we gave her a new opportunity that would slightly change her direction and position within our company. Because our company is growing, we need people to fill specific roles. And while she's failed miserably at some roles, she's excelled at others. The responsibility you hold in their Upper Realm is either to provide positions in your Lower Realm in which employees are perfect fits or to eliminate their current positions and free them to pursue work elsewhere. Thankfully in this case my husband and I don't know how to quit starting new businesses, so we were able to find a role that's a perfect fit for her and put her in it. This also gives her the power of choice. She can now choose to accept her new position in the company or find work elsewhere. It removes the burden from us and places the power of her future and direction in her hands. And the ultimate reward may be that you discover hidden talents your employees and independent contractors didn't even recognize they had!

The Obscure Lower Realm Inhabitants

You may think that if someone gives you money for a product or service that person is in your Upper Realm and holds some sort of power over you. This is a Normalcy Trap for many service providers. Let me get one point *very* clear: Just because currency changes hands, it does *not* give others power over how you spend your time, money, and energy! Your clients are in your Lower Realm. They do not hold authority over you unless you invite them to become obscure Upper Realm inhabitants. So many new entrepreneurs, especially those who have worked for years in more corporate-style settings, are stuck in the mindset that clients equal bosses and therefore you must do everything they demand of you. The truth is that clients hire you to do something for them. They choose you for a reason and it's *your* choice to do the work or not. If after you set clear boundaries with a client he or she becomes demanding, belittling, or worse, that person is a bully.

In our online training businesses, Tony and I have fired a few of our customers due to their habit of continually trying to hold authority over how we choose to run our businesses or spend our time. In some cases they become so abusive, we've not only fired and refunded them, but we've reported them to all our friends in the business who then removed the bullies from their lists and blocked them from purchasing in the future. In this day of the internet it's incredibly easy for people to hide behind their computer screens, assume they have some sort of power over others, then abuse that assumption by bullying product and service providers into giving more time, energy, and resources than are included in their purchase.

If a client continues to push at you in this way after receiving the terms of your agreement, this is when you have to take the position of authority and do something that may scare you... bite the bullet, and issue that refund and fire them. By not taking proactive action and continually bending to their will and desires, you are allowing them to continuously inhabit your personal Upper Realm instead of remaining in your Lower Realm, which is where they belong. This action will lead to you losing sleep and resenting taking on anyone else in the future, which can actually kill your business.

I once lost several months to such a client. While I had red flags in our first meeting, I didn't heed those internal warnings and took her on as a client anyway. Over the next few months nothing my team did was good enough for her. She kept demanding more of my time than I had included in her package and would not honor our written contract, even when I copied and pasted it back to her. She kept saying that I "said" something different than what she signed, and at one point she went so far as to ignore the fact that she had signed the paperwork and accuse me of forging her signature, when she had signed everything

PAY CLOSE ATTENTION TO ANY RED FLAGS

in front of three other people at a marketing event. I finally had enough of losing sleep and fretting over it. When I decided to let her go, I drained one of my accounts and refunded her over $8,000. While it scared the crap out of me and I honestly didn't know how I would buy groceries that week, the freedom I felt at firing her as a client made my heart sing. I felt such a sudden shift, change, and weight lifted that I approached my business with a different energy. And within two days I'd signed not one, but *two* brand new $10,000 clients.

Letting go of dead weight in your life can be one of the scariest experiences you'll ever have to face. Whether it's a problem employee or contractor or a problem client, once you set boundaries with those in your Lower Realm on what's expected of them and how you expect to be treated and cull those who blatantly refuse to follow your guidelines, your business could experience the incredible growth spurt you've been longing for.

REMEMBER WHO IS IN CONTROL OF YOUR BUSINESS

It's important to remember who is in control of your business. Is your business *yours* or your clients'? Obscure inhabitants of these realms can be a confusing lot. Take this book for example. I hired a couple of editors to polish this manuscript and looked to their expertise, which temporarily placed them in my personal Upper Realm, and by default as their client I would be in their Lower Realm. If I made unwarranted demands of them, I would be bullying them and because they are in control of their businesses they have the authority to let me go and leave me to my own grammatically incorrect devices. At the same time, money is exchanging hands, so I have a level of expectation for the service they will provide. In this instance I am temporarily in *their* Upper Realms as I'm telling them what to do with my book, and that is as far as my obscure habitat in their Upper Realms extends. At the same time, they are in my Upper Realm as they are giving me advice for my book and it's my *choice* to accept that advice. If I choose not to accept it then it is my responsibility to deal with the consequences. Since there are consequences involved in my decision regarding how I act on their guidance, they are in my Upper Realm as invited guests.

This scenario creates a bridge across Realms where the boundaries are the parameters of the project. We each inhabit each other's Upper and Lower Realms at the same time, but for different purposes with a different set of boundaries on each end of the bridge. Once the project is complete, that bridge is removed and we no longer inhabit either of each other's spaces.

If you have created a Normalcy Trap of Lower Realm abuse and allowed those in your Lower Realm to cross boundaries into your Upper Realm, it's time for you to take control of your business, life, and respect—and discipline them. This is the first step toward achieving a Mindset of Mastery in your business which, when combined with the other two realms, will make you and your mission unstoppable.

16

The Mindset of Mastery

To effectively tap into the Lower Realm of Asskickonomics you need to develop a Mindset of Mastery. This mindset will enable you to troubleshoot problem situations and to resolve conflicts with employees and VAs. It's a solid commitment you make to being the best *you* in your business and personal life. Because how you treat your family and friends is a direct reflection of how you treat those "beneath" you in the Lower Realm. Bring your best to *everyone* around you, not just those you're closest to or feel the most comfortable with. I'm not asking you to do anything easy. To the contrary, being the best *you* every moment in every aspect of your life can be daunting. There may be a tendency to be too hard on yourself. To continually wonder why you don't measure up… to your own standards. To push yourself beyond your physical limits. So you must find the balance and realize that when you strip every title away—parent, boss, entrepreneur, friend, etc.—what you're left with is *you*. And *you* may be a superhero; yet you must still adhere to the physical limitations of being human.

How do you find this balance? By facing every decision and situation with a question: What is the best way to do X? You must understand that the best answer you come up with may change as you continue to learn new strategies and implement new tools. Recognize that the key to being good at anything is to put in the *time* even if you don't feel like you have the talent. Any skill can be learned. I personally taught myself BASIC coding in High School and HTML in college. Yet both those skills are useless to me now as I've made the decision to be bad at tech. Because that's really what it is, a decision not to understand tech, even though I know that if I simply put in the *time* I could learn it. However, you also need to know where your genius lies. My genius is in my creativity. My ability to see patterns and pull solutions from complex situations. It's not in coding, so I choose to tap into my Lower Realm and hire tech people to help me out in that area. I've learned that it's important to put in the time to improve my strengths, not to focus on my weaknesses and attempt to strengthen them. Because what you'll soon realize is that the answer to "What is the best way to do X" may actually be to outsource X to someone who's better at it than you will ever be… and to trust those in your Lower Realm to kick ass for you and your business.

> # FOCUS ON IMPROVING YOUR STRENGTHS AND TAP INTO YOUR LOWER REALM TO IMPROVE YOUR WEAKNESSES

When you approach the various tasks on your to-do list with a mastery mindset, the time you spend doing those tasks becomes much more productive. There have been many times when we've been traveling and my husband has had to do work for himself that my VAs in my business normally handle for me. He's bent over his computer gathering documents and setting things up and I'm hanging out in the hot tub brainstorming new ideas. While he's very good at those tasks and can probably do them faster than the average VA, his time is better freed to focus on other things when he allows a VA to take on those tasks for him. By answering the question, "What is the best way to do X" with the power of those more competent in that X task than you are, you'll increase your ability to showcase your stronger talents.

You may choose to take on a task and learn it inside and out because you enjoy it and that's awesome! This will increase your self-confidence and your competence in that area and once you've mastered it, these motivators will spill over into other areas of your life and business. Mastering a task (whether you're naturally good at it or not) is always a good thing. It also enables you to know when someone on your team may be doing something wrong. I rarely run the register for our toy store anymore. My natural gifts and talents are best used in other areas, like marketing and team building. So while I mastered things like opening and closing the register, I quickly turned those tasks over to my employees. When employees make mistakes I can tell, because I know how the system is supposed to work. This enables me to talk to them about it and help them improve their skills.

Think of your business like a pyramid. If you're always doing the tasks of laying the foundation, you'll never have the chance to build the next phase of steps. Or the next. And you'll never progress to installing the point. The only way to build a pyramid is by incorporating the Lower Realm of Asskickonomics whenever and wherever it makes sense and to own your own greatness in your natural talents. Most entrepreneurs I've met think they have to wear all the hats and do everything in their businesses themselves. Then if I'm talking to women entrepreneurs, their responsibilities also extend to taking care of sick kids, getting them ready for school, making meals for everyone, and generally trying to pull off the impossible, just to rinse and repeat it the next day, the next week, and so on. It's no wonder so many women entrepreneurs

ENABLE YOURSELF TO EXCEL WHERE YOU NEED TO AND STEP BACK WHERE YOU DON'T

get burned out! And worse yet, this situation often becomes a Normalcy Trap for these entrepreneurs as they continue these habits year after year. By activating the Mindset of Mastery, you enable yourself to excel where you need to and to step back where you don't. In this way you own your own greatness, which as described by my friend and the founder of the ground-breaking personal development program Radical Leadership, Therese Kienest, is "the true definition of humility."

Humility is essential when dealing with the Lower Realm. If those under your authority continually see you as someone better than them who's always doing everything they should and re-doing what they've done, they'll feel like it's impossible to measure up. However, when you own your own greatness in your strengths and allow *them* to *own theirs* to help build your organization, you're showing them the power of humility and giving them a vested interest in helping to make your entrepreneurial dreams and goals come true.

Entrepreneurial or Purposeful?

I've used the word "entrepreneur" in some form a lot in this book. One-hundred and four times to be exact. Yet there's a difference between being entrepreneurial and purposeful. By defining yourself as only an entrepreneur, you're doing everything as well as you can. Which is fine and there's a higher level at which you can play. Being purposeful means you do something as well as *it can be done*. This means being willing to change what you're doing to get better results. As I said way back in Chapter 1, until the pain of staying the same becomes greater than the pain of change, nothing will change.

Entrepreneurial people complete tasks with enthusiasm, energy, and their natural abilities. What those who operate in this way don't realize is that success has a natural ceiling. Once they've reached a level of achievement, they move on to something else. This is why you often see entrepreneurs juggle several different startup businesses and why some people do just enough of a task to learn what they want and then move on to something else. I have a friend who has operated much of her life this way. She was visiting me for about a week and she asked me to teach her how to make stained glass, since I'd recently re-acquired all the tools. I agreed, so we went through the process of creating a pattern, choosing the best parts of the glass for that pattern, cutting the glass, and then grinding it for the pieces to fit together. She was about two thirds of the way through the grinding process when she stopped and said she was done. Being her instructor in that art, I knew what was left to make a finished piece so I asked her if she wanted to learn those other things. Her answer was, "Nope, I've learned all I've wanted to. I'm ready for something else." She approached the art of creating a stained-glass piece in an wantre-preneurial way rather than a purposeful way.

Purposeful people challenge that success ceiling. They don't accept their own limitations or even their own desires. Instead, they are always on the lookout for new ways to push through. It's entre-preneurs who approach their goals from the stand-point of being purposeful who achieve break-throughs in technology and

PURPOSE CHALLENGES THE SUCCESS CEILING

accomplishments beyond their natural abilities. These are the innovators—those who truly come up with new ideas that have the power to change the very shape of the planet we inhabit. These are the Nikola Teslas, the Walt Disneys, and the Steve Jobses of the world. They're never satisfied with where they currently are—they're always looking for ways to improve. Whether that's to improve a product or a service or to build the biggest amusement park on the planet, the only way they could reach these achievements was to approach *everything* they did with purpose. This means that sometimes you have to say no to good things to make room for the purposeful amazing things.

DON'T PUT LIMITS ON WHAT YOU'RE CAPABLE OF DOING

This ties right back into the Mindset of Mastery. As you embrace the amazing, you'll find that the good things may still need to get done. And to do them in the best possible way, you may find that you need to rely on someone else. Don't put limits on what you're capable of doing, including building a team of like-minded Lower Realm inhabitants to help you to build your dream. Don't ever settle for "good enough." Instead ask yourself how you can do even better. Years ago I had a part-time job working for an art training studio. One of my first tasks was to take samples of our work—high-end wall faux finishes—and to create an artistic display of them on the wall. I laid out what I felt was a brilliant plan on the floor of the studio, a task that took me about three hours to complete. When my boss Barb walked in, she commended me for how great it looked. I felt my chest begin to swell with pride. Then I quickly deflated as she said, "Now pick it all up and do it all over again." I panicked. First, I was attached to the work I'd spent most of the day doing. And second, I felt it was "good enough." That's when she told me, "One of the most important business lessons I ever learned was that in order to make something better, you have to destroy what you've already done." I re-created the design in less than an hour and you know what? She was right! Not only was the new version much better than the first (which she allowed me to put up on the wall), but it took me a fraction of the original time to do. Part of the issue was that I was over-analyzing everything, coming at it with enthusiasm and energy, yes, but tapping only into my natural abilities instead of pushing the limits. She forced me to shatter that glass ceiling of success I initially felt and to tap into something even more powerful within myself—purpose.

I could have gotten frustrated at her response, walked out, and said I'd had enough. But I chose to embrace her idea of doing it over from scratch (and keep my job). When you stay open to new ideas from those in your Lower Realm and challenge *them* to adopt the Mindset of Mastery in everything they do as well, you will be able to hold each other accountable and truly activate the third and final realm of Asskickonomics in your team, as Barb did with me. You will hit that ceiling of success and that's your chance to explore new options. How can you reach past it? How can you raise it? Every time you reach a goal, "up" it. Give yourself another, greater challenge. Stretch yourself to new heights of success and encourage those in your Lower Realm to follow suit with their own responsibilities. Once you make The Mindset of Mastery a natural habit and way of living, you'll experience extraordinary results!

17

Take Massive, Intentional Action

All experienced entrepreneurs will tell you that the primary reason they're successful isn't because of the courses they take, the tools they invest in, the employees they hire, or even the money they invest in start-ups and growth. No, the primary reason they're successful is because they know what they want and they take massive, intentional action to get it. In Chapter 2 of his book *The ABCs of Success*, Bob Proctor says, "There are risks and costs to action. But they are far less than the long-range risks of comfortable inaction. Action is a great restorer and builder of confidence. Inaction is not only the result, but the cause, of fear. Perhaps the action you take will be successful; perhaps different action or adjustments will have to follow. But any action is better than no action at all. Doubt, of whatever kind, can be ended by action alone."

All the training, resources, and money in the world won't give you the success you desire unless you *act* on your ideas. And to act on your ideas you must be *extremely clear* in what you want. Unless you know what you want, SOS will steer you in multiple directions and you'll end up right back where you started with no more money in the bank to show for it. When you're clear on what you want and set goals to reach that ultimate dream, then all the "shinies" in the world can come at you and you'll be able confidently to say, "No" or, "Not right now" as you focus on your next action step.

What Do I Want?

This is the most important question for you to get clear on. Asking that question of yourself is the only way for you to drill down into your ultimate dreams and goals, no matter how big or small they may be. The more specific you are, the less God, the Universe (whatever your beliefs), and helpful humans will have to guess what you want and will be able to step in to make the magic happen for you. It's also how you can attract amazingness into your life! Here are a couple of examples of how I have attracted amazingness into my own life just by being clear on what I wanted.

> **WHEN YOU'RE CLEAR ON WHAT YOU WANT, YOU'LL ATTRACT AMAZINGNESS INTO YOUR LIFE**

While my husband and I were visiting my favorite rock shop on our honeymoon, we went out to dinner with the owners who were my friends. Our toy store was still a "someday" idea and we had other dreams that were starting to solidify in our minds for the future. However, one thing was becoming very clear in what we wanted, which is that our ultimate "Rome," the place every road we're building now leads up to, would require a lot of life-sized dinosaurs. Not knowing how or even where to look for these creatures, we asked my friend Doc (Doc's Rocks Gem Mine in Blowing Rock, NC) where he got his life-sized young T-Rex. Long story short, we ended up coming home from our honeymoon with a delivery of ten life-sized dinosaurs, many of them animatronic... which have now become featured attractions and exhibits at our toy store.

BE OPEN AND READY FOR WHAT YOU WANT

As I transitioned my online training business into more of a consulting space, I wanted a retreat-style place where I could go to be with my ideas without distracting cellphone notifications. Now I'm the first to admit that I have a technology addiction. Believe me, I know that it's a lot easier to say turn off your notifications than it is to actually *do* it. Between my Apple Watch, iPhone, iPad Pro, MacBook Pro, and my husband's assortment of the same, it's hard for us to get away and completely unplug... unless we're on an airplane with no Wi-Fi. The only time we can focus on a project without those notification distractions is by forced unplugging.

In addition to a retreat for ourselves, I also wanted a space where I could take my VIP consulting clients to where *they* wouldn't be distracted by all those dings and lights going off every few seconds as we dialed in their business plans and goals. My husband and I talked about it and decided to keep our eyes open for the perfect opportunity. Little did I know that someone I knew had property for sale. We looked at the site and as I ship this manuscript off to the editor, our realtor is working on drawing up the paperwork on the best deal we could ever have imagined. And even better than the deal we made? There's *zero* cell service in that area. Nada. Nothin'. No towers, no carriers, no networks. Even the internet can be a little sketchy. What better property to fall into our laps at the *perfect* time, all because we were open, ready, and *clear* on what we wanted!

What Do YOU Want?

It's time for you to get clear on what *you* want. The easiest way to do this is to start with the question—asked of you by someone else. Have a friend or family member do this exercise with you. Start with having them ask you, "What do you want?" Then say it as quickly as possible. Write down whatever comes out of your mouth. Impulse here is key, as impulse is emotion-brain driven and taps into the creative centers of your cerebral cortex. This eliminates the logical analyzing side, which often leaves you paralyzed wondering, "Well, what *do* I want?"

After you write it down, ask yourself:

Is it clear?

Do you need to explain it anymore? Is it something you can clearly communicate to someone else, such as an influencer who can help you get it done?

Is it specific?

Just like goals, what you want should be specific. Believe it or not, specifics are how the success of your want becoming reality will manifest in your life. It may feel like the opposite is true, but trust me it isn't. Just like when you're shopping for a new car and suddenly you start seeing that car in the exact color and configurations that you want—everywhere—your mind will use this same filter with your specific want to filter out anything that doesn't perfectly align with it, leaving you open only to the most absolute *perfect* solutions.

Is it big enough?

Nobody ever accused innovators at the level of Tesla, Einstein, Ford, and more recently, Jobs, of dreaming small. If anything, society thought their desires were *so big* they were "crazy" and discounted them saying, "It will never last." Yet because these innovators all took intentional, massive action and didn't stop working toward their ultimate dreams, they took their success straight to the bank.

The "Is it big enough?" question is where so many wantrepreneurs get stuck in "want" and never make it to "ent." They create a Normalcy Trap of "almost big enough," because to think bigger scares the living shit out of them. Which is precisely where you want to be! If what you want doesn't scare you a little, it's not big enough to be magical once it happens. It's not big enough to make you stretch yourself and what you're capable of to see it come to fruition. If what you want is big enough, it will *require* change in yourself and you'll find it necessary to surround yourself with like-minded people who share and encourage your vision. It may require a change in your relationships. And it will probably take massive amounts of energy and action to happen.

> # IF WHAT YOU WANT DOESN'T SCARE YOU A LITTLE, IT'S NOT BIG ENOUGH

Do other people challenge your vision? Do they encourage you to think even bigger than you already are? If they do, your want is not yet big enough.

An Example: My Clear Wants

When we opened our toy store in July of 2017, I knew I had to get clear on the specifics of my want for the new enterprise, otherwise the store would end up just like every other struggling retailer in the typical downtown. So I made a list of what I wanted the store to be, including the experiences I wanted customers and children to have, and my financial goals. My wants were:

To sell **unique toys and books not found elsewhere** in the region, including in big box stores. The interesting thing about this want is that our store has become the predecessor for toys later stocked on big box shelves. While this annoys me a little, I take pride in the fact that we had it stocked for many months before the big boxes got it in. We stay on top of educational toy trends and are told several times per day how much our customers love the uniqueness in the toys our store offers. In fact one family of four generations bought the fourth generation only child one single gift from a big box store for Christmas—something we don't sell—and *all* her other gifts came from our shop. The support we've received for the time we spend seeking out and ordering unique toys and books has propelled us toward greater success.

To **create an environment** that makes kids say, "WOW!" and adults stop in their tracks and say, "Holy shit." I can't tell you how many adults I've heard hold their tongues when they enter our store, as we try to keep a G-rated environment. From the museum-grade animatronic dinosaur exhibit in the front display window to the life-sized, nine-and-a-half-foot-long deinonychus we've named Phil (with which guests can take selfies) showcased in front of a museum-quality forest-print backdrop, trees, grass, and even a waterfall and geodes, to the twisting vines twinkling with fairy lights and fairy light globes to the swooping fabric filled with twinkle lights across the back half of the ceiling, our goal of creating a "wonderland" was accomplished the first time I heard a child scream, "WOW! Look, mom, REAL DINOSAURS!" Our display window exhibit has brought in hundreds of first-time customers who have already become regulars. All because I started with a clear want to create an environment instead of just to stock a bunch of products in a pretty store.

To **bring play back to adults** as well as encouraging off-screen, battery-free play for kids, with tangible toys and games. Often a family with young children will enter our store and an adult will say, "Now don't touch ANYTHING!" To which I've trained my staff to gently respond to these often tired and frustrated adults that our environment is one of play and fun, filled with hands-on toy tester stations where kids can interact with the toys and adults can remember the freedom play gave them as children. Every single time a frustrated adult has been given this explanation, I've seen a visual load lift off their shoulders, they smile, and it's become something we've heard from hundreds of people, "I just LOVE how you have toys out we can touch, feel, and play with!" We even have an entire department of staff at the bank next door regularly visit to play on their breaks and to take home a new desk toy.

To make the amount of money necessary to **break even on expenses within the first 60 days**. To **double that amount in the next 90 days**. This clearly specific want is unheard of in retail to the point that most won't even utter it out loud, even if they have the fleeting thought of it. It's an ambitious, BIG want. In fact we were told by other retailers and toy store owners that it would be about two years before we would break even. Guess what? Declare what you want and attract results... we broke even in 60 days. Within the next three months we were in the black... *before Christmas season started*. In less than six months we did one-and-a-half-times in gross revenue what other independent toy store owners told us the average *established* store generates in a *year*. While I do believe a lot of our success has to do with our knowledge in marketing, I honestly believe it has even more to do with everything I've laid out in this book.

MAKE WHAT YOU WANT CLEAR AND SPECIFIC

The Unseen Enemy

As with any big idea there lies an unseen enemy to you getting what you want, even after you're clear on what that want is. This enemy may seem obvious to you, especially since I already mentioned it back in Chapter 3. The unseen enemy, Making It Hard Syndrome, has many symptoms including (and certainly not limited to) procrastination, perfectionism, gut feelings that something isn't "right," overthinking, continuously asking questions instead of taking action, overwhelm, discouragement, fear, dread, shame, and asking questions when you already *know* the answers.

There are several indicators to know if you have this problem. Do you:

⇨ Feel guilty for living life the way you *want* to?

⇨ Habitually "help out" toxic people (effectively enabling their behavior)?

⇨ Tend to only look at the negative in a situation?

⇨ Constantly see what you *don't* have rather than what you *do* have?

⇨ Worry that people will steal your ideas?

⇨ Focus on the future or past and rarely the present?

⇨ Subscribe to an "all or nothing" mentality of extremes?

⇨ Find it impossible to get past your mistakes?

⇨ Think everyone on Facebook is happy... All. The. Time?

⇨ Often think of the worst-case scenario?

⇨ Suffer from habitual indecision?

⇨ Experience a positive result or event then default to asking, "What's the catch?"

The chances are if you often experience any of the above indicators, you're making things harder than they need to be. That list above is full of "reasons" (excuses) why you shouldn't achieve what you want, much less actually want it to begin with. So if these are just excuses, what actually causes us to make it hard? If these "reasons" are keeping you from achieving your ultimate passion dream, then there's something even deeper in your life at work holding you back. Whether that's undervaluing yourself

WATCH OUT FOR THE TRAP OF "IF IT'S NOT HARD, IT'S NOT WORTH DOING"

and your abilities or a false belief bred by society that if it's not hard it's not worth doing, this underlying anti-motivation issue provides an "out" when things go wrong. Because if you have a good reason not to go after what you want, then if it goes south you've avoided the pain so that must be good, right? It's a convoluted way to avoid the discomfort you just imagined into existence.

This is exactly how role-playing the worst case scenario affects us. We make it hard by imagining the worst that can happen with a major decision, then get paralyzed by fear. And if or when you finally *do* have a breakthrough and accomplish what you want, you've now done the "impossible" and triumphed over your own issues that were blocking you from moving forward. If you let this event become a pattern that continues, the false sense of heroism you experience can lead to a repeating pattern and Normalcy Trap of self-sabotage, just so you can swoop in and save the day again.

So now I have another question for you… What are you getting out of it? When you make something hard, whether it's accomplishing a task or setting a goal that will get you closer to your ultimate want, there's something you're getting out of it. It may be attention, accolades, recognition for a job well done, etc. Whatever it is, the harder the want is to achieve the greater the achievement, so by default the greater the reward. And every time you repeat this cycle it usually gets harder and harder to achieve your want, so the reward becomes greater and greater, which also increases the thrill of accomplishment. See the potential spiral into the Normalcy Trap of self-sabotage?

The Solution

My good friend and awesome leadership coach Therese Sparkins often says, "If you don't get what you want legitimately, you'll get what you want illegitimately." I've found this to be so true for myself! I'm an only child (we'll use this as my excuse for the following story). And I admit I *love* being the center of attention. I like recognition and I hate behind-the-scenes support work. I want to be on stage, front and center, the one people point at and say, "Wow, you inspired me!" Now society tried to teach me that being the center of attention was selfish and wrong, so I acted out to get what I wanted. I'd create drama, blow up, have a meltdown; whatever it took to get attention. Then I discovered the world of speaking, coaching, training, and consulting. I *excelled* in that space. Why? Because I *wanted* the spotlight. And when I began (and continued) to get the spotlight legitimately as an instructor and leader, the drama in my life faded. My husband often tells the story of when we first met, six years before we dated. I was a hot mess back then and as he describes it, "I saw her and was like *hell no*, I can't take all of... [waving his hands in the general direction of where I would have stood in the room] *that*." He was right! I craved what I wanted without even realizing it was a want, and I sought out any means I possibly could to get it.

Fast-forward through years of coaching and personal growth and the man who couldn't handle "that" asked me to marry him. If you ask him what changed he'll say, "She grew up." And that's definitely true. I grew up to discover how I could get what I wanted legitimately and how I could use that influence to help, inspire, and motivate others on a much bigger scale. It took me years to learn that getting what you want doesn't have to be hard. All you have to do is give yourself permission for it to be easy! Be aware of what you physically feel when you begin to hit resistance to your want. Is it triggered by something? The key is in awareness... always being aware of how you feel, how you react, and how you respond to anything that seems to be keeping you from getting what you want, especially if that something is yourself. Get a coach, accountability partner, or at bare minimum someone who will support you and point out when you're making something hard. The more you notice *when* you're doing it, the more you'll get into a habit of noticing the warning signs—the hairs standing up on the back of your neck, if you will—and be able to stop it before it gets out of hand and keeps you from accomplishing your dream. Then finally, make a conscious decision to stop making shit hard. STOP IT. You may think that sounds easier said than done, but that's just it! It is supposed to be easy!

When you feel like you're starting to fall into your Normalcy Trap of making it hard to get what you want, ask yourself a few questions. First ask, "Is there an easier way?" I know that question sounds a bit obvious, but you'll be surprised how you may answer it! If there's not an easier way, ask, "Is this goal just too high?" Maybe you are not quite ready for what you're striving toward. And that's OK! There's probably a reason you're unaware of what's keeping you from making progress. It's OK to change a goal and shift into a new direction—as long as it's not just a reason to procrastinate because

> # MAKE A CONSCIOUS DECISION TO STOP MAKING SHIT HARD

you're getting a little uncomfortable. If the goal is well within your power to reach, ask, "What am I getting out of making this hard and getting stuck?" and re-read the previous section of this chapter again. You may not like the hard truths that will appear as you dive deeper into the answers to these questions, and asking them is the first step toward breakthrough to an easier time of getting what you want... and ultimately reaching your goals to make your passion dream a reality.

Above all, remember easy is actually *normal*. We've been taught differently and it's time to take a stand for easy. Don't make things harder than they have to be. This world is yours to impact and I'm standing with you as you read these final sentences, cheering you on to take massive, intentional action! You were *made* for this moment! So put your ideas into action, embrace the entrepreneur you're meant to be, activate all three Realms of Asskickonomics, embrace your dreams, and step onto your solid path of success!

ACKNOWLEDGEMENTS

A special thanks goes out to the following people who all made the writing of this book possible:

My incredible and supportive entrepreneur husband Tony, who designed the book cover and listened to me read chapters to him as I wrote. Your honest feedback and mad design skills made this book the best it could possibly be. And I'll always love our crazy 3 a.m. business brainstorms. We have the best couple-entrepreneur relationship in the universe!

Tanner Larsson and Vinnie Fisher for sharing your vulnerability with me in a way that inspired me to write this book. Your openness and honesty helped me discover my message to the world.

My mom Lindy Stein, who listened as I read the entire book out loud from start to finish while she suffered from the flu. Your perseverence to live your best life and run your own business full time is a daily inspiration to me. I'm still amazed when you take my advice.

My editor Gordon, and friends over at Edit911 including CEO Marc D. Baldwin. Your consistent feedback with suggestions on how to make the book stronger gave it the fine-tuning it needed.

My proof reader Diana Henderson, whose sharp eyes caught the few remaining inconsistencies in this book. No book is 100% perfect, but with you on my team this one has come damn close.

My business coach Kamin, who worked with me while I was writing this book to kick my ass, help shift my mindset, and remind me to take my own advice. You, my friend, are an angel.

All of my amazing friends who agreed to review this book and sent in glowing feedback and reviews that brought me to my knees. You made me beam with pride and wipe a few tears from my eyes.

My customers who invested in the book before even really knowing what it was about. Your faith in me and my message means more to me than you'll ever know.

ABOUT THE AUTHOR

Kristen Joy Laidig decided she was "unemployable" at the tender age of six when she started her first business making and selling pet rocks with nothing but a Sharpie® marker, gravel, and ingenuity.

A serial entrepreneur, in 2003 she turned her life-long love of writing into a full-time career teaching authors and entrepreneurs how to create books that bring them business and turning authors into successful authorpreneurs through her internationally-known brand, The Book Ninja®.

After discovering how to thrive through chronic illness and an autoimmune disorder, Kristen went on to write and publish 18 Kindle books in 18 weeks (authoring a total of over 32 books), start over 50 publishing companies, publish over 200 books and e-books, teach hundreds of webinars, coach thousands of authors from idea to published, build a livelihood from negative $300-a-month to a multi-six-figure business, study martial arts at four different schools with three disciplines, earn her black belt in karate, get her conceal-carry license and eat way too much chocolate.

She currently changes lives through her students... one published message at a time, invests in start-up companies, manages her own book and toy store *Toy Box Gifts & Wonder*® in the heart of her newfound hometown, Chambersburg, PA, is in the start-up phase of at least three new businesses at any given time (including she and her husband's next retail store, *Nerdvana Outpost*, also in downtown Chambersburg), and consults existing business owners who are ready to level up their game.

Besides on her website at KristenJoysBlog.com, she can also be found building relationships online at her second home in Facebookland (Facebook.com/thekristenjoy), brainstorming business ideas in her hot tub, playing with her two ragdoll kitties, or roaming the toy aisles with her man at Target hunting down toys for themselves and their cats.

LET'S HANG OUT!

Join my *The Business Ninja Entrepreneurs* support group on Facebook and let's hang out and create awesomeness together!

Facebook.com/Groups/BusinessNinja

OTHER BOOKS

Be sure to add these companion books to your kick-ass business book collection!

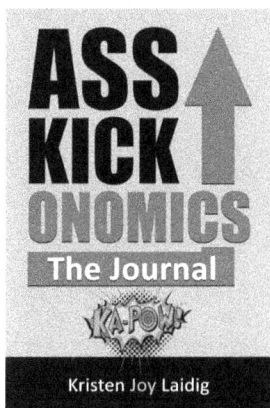

Designed to be used alongside the book you're holding right now, *Asskickonomics: The Journal* is your personal 90-day tracking guide to help you effectively play in all three Realms of Asskickonomics every day and create the life and business of your dreams.

With sections specific for setting your big 90-Day Passion Goal, business brainstorms, tracking each day's success and action steps, this book is essential for you to be the successful entrepreneur you desire!

Asskickonomics: The Workbook is specially designed to hold your hand through action steps outlined in the book you're holding now. Each section in *The Workbook* follows each chapter in this book and will take you on a journey as you read *Asskickonomics* to deep-dive into the material and incorporate it into your business.

Perfect for group studies and workshops, *Asskickonomics: The Workbook* is the essential companion to the other two books in this series.

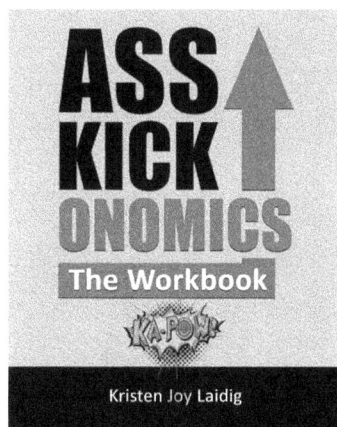

Get both companion books at Asskickonomics.com, Amazon.com or wherever fine books are sold!

www.ingramcontent.com/pod-product-compliance
Lightning Source LLC
Chambersburg PA
CBHW071605210326
41597CB00019B/3415